# Cambridge Lower Secondary

# English as a Second Language

## STAGE 8:  WORKBOOK

Anna Osborn

**Series Editor:** Nick Coates

William Collins' dream of knowledge for all began with the publication of his first book in 1819.

A self-educated mill worker, he not only enriched millions of lives, but also founded a flourishing publishing house. Today, staying true to this spirit, Collins books are packed with inspiration, innovation and practical expertise. They place you at the centre of a world of possibility and give you exactly what you need to explore it.

Collins. Freedom to teach.

Published by Collins
An imprint of HarperCollins*Publishers*
The News Building
1 London Bridge Street
London
SE1 9GF

HarperCollins*Publishers*
Macken House, 39/40 Mayor Street Upper,
Dublin 1, D01 C9W8, Ireland

Browse the complete Collins catalogue at
**www.collins.co.uk**

10 9 8 7

ISBN 978-0-00-836686-5

British Library Cataloguing-in-Publication Data
A catalogue record for this publication is available from the British Library.

Author: Anna Osborn
Series Editor: Nick Coates
Project manager: Lucy Hobbs
Development editor: Helen King
Product manager: Lucy Cooper
Cover designer: Gordon McGlip
Cover illustrator: Maria Herbert-Liew
Typesetter: Jouve India Private Ltd
Production controller: Lyndsey Rogers
Printed in India by Multivista Global Pvt.Ltd.

MIX
Paper | Supporting responsible forestry
FSC™ C007454

This book contains FSC™ certified paper and other controlled sources to ensure responsible forest management.

For more information visit: www.harpercollins.co.uk/green

## Acknowledgements

Key: t = top, b = bottom, l = left, r = right, c = centre

p5 Fer Gregory/Shutterstock, p10 Monkey Business Images/Shutterstock, p12 bezikus/Shutterstock, p13 Phase4Studios/Shutterstock, p16t Ermolaev Alexander/Shutterstock, p16c GUNDAM_Ai/Shutterstock, p16c Monkey Business Images/Shutterstock, p16b NewFabrika/Shutterstock, p17l lzf/Shutterstock, p17r Billion Photos/Shutterstock, p18 fotoinfot/Shutterstock, p20 wavebreakmedia/Shutterstock, p23 Billion Photos/Shutterstock, p26 Mike Focus/Shutterstock, p32tl Ammit Jack/Shutterstock, p32tc AlexZaitsev/Shutterstock, p32tr djgis/Shutterstock, p32bl blvdone/Shutterstock, p32bc Tisha 85/Shutterstock, p32br Nonchanon/Shutterstock, p32b iFerol/Shutterstock, p33 Wim Hoek/Shutterstock, p36 Konstanttin/Shutterstock, p42 Iakov Filimonov/Shutterstock, p46 DVARG/Shutterstock, p48 Irina Nartova/Shuttestock, p53 Wang An Qi/Shutterstock, p58tl wavebreakmedia/Shutterstock, p58tc Toa55/Shutterstock, p58tr Likoper/Shutterstock, p58bl Rawpixel.com/Shutterstock, p58bc Cameron Whitman/Shutterstock, p58br leungchopan/Shutterstock, p69 Dean Drobot/Shutterstock, p80 Peeradach R/Shutterstock

The publishers gratefully acknowledge the permission granted to reproduce the copyright material in this book. Every effort has been made to trace copyright holders and to obtain their permission for the use of copyright material. The publishers will gladly receive any information enabling them to rectify any error or omission at the first opportunity.

With thanks to the following teachers and schools for reviewing materials in development: Hawar International School; Khushnuma Gandhi, HVB Global Academy; Judith Hughes, International School of Budapest; Babara Khan, Jankidevi Public School.

# Contents

# Introduction

The Collins *Cambridge Lower Secondary English as a Second Language* course consists of a Student's Book and Workbook for students for each of Stages 7, 8 and 9. A Teacher's Guide includes other lesson ideas and materials, and your teacher will also have access to the recorded listening materials.

The *Stage 8 Workbook* directly supports the Student's Book with a Workbook unit for every unit in the Student's Book. The units are numbered in the same way and the sequence of activities in the Workbook follow those of the Student's Book. Each Workbook activity also has a page reference to the relevant activity in the Student's Book to make the link between the two books clear.

The Workbook units give you further practice of the grammar, vocabulary and skills taught in the Student's Book. It also contains activities designed either for support or for extension work. For example, to accompany the Student's Book reading activities, the Workbook includes *Reading: comprehension* and *Reading: thinking about the text* activities. The *comprehension* activity can be used for further practice of basic comprehension. The Workbook *thinking about the text* activity focuses on more advanced reading skills such as implied meaning, critical analysis and application, so you can use it to challenge yourself. The *Focus on Grammar* section at the back of the Workbook provides a short summary of the key grammar points for Stage 8 which you can use for reference.

*For teachers*

*Registered Cambridge International Schools benefit from high-quality programmes, assessments and a wide range of support so that teachers can effectively deliver Cambridge Lower Secondary. Visit www.cambridgeinternational.org/lowersecondary to find out more.*

# 1 Film and drama

## Vocabulary: types of film

Complete the crossword.

**Across**
**1** a serious film
**3** a film with singing
**5** a film about real life
**6** a film set in the future (2 words)

**Down**
**2** a cartoon (2 words)
**4** a funny film

## Reading: comprehension

SB p.9

Answer the questions.
**1** Which film is a sequel? _____
**2** Who wrote *Tom's Dream*? _____
**3** What year is *Don't Look Back* set in? _____
**4** Where does the main character in *Mouse on Goal* live? _____
**5** Who directed *Sweet Fun*? _____
**6** When is *Tom's Dream* set? _____

## Reading: thinking about the text

SB p.9

**Reading tip**

Looking at the adjectives that writers use is a good way of understanding their opinions. They will use positive adjectives to describe things they like and negative adjectives to describe things that they don't like.

**1** Answer the questions.
    **1** Which of the films does the writer of the reviews like?

_____

**2** What adjectives do they use that make you understand this?

_____

_____

**3** Which of the films does the writer *not* like?

_____

**4** What adjectives do they use that make you understand this?

_____

**2** What's your opinion of the films in these reviews? Complete the sentences.

**1** I'd like to watch _____ (name of film) because _____.

**2** I wouldn't like to watch _____ (name of film) because _____
_____.

## Vocabulary: talking about films
SB p.10

**1** Complete the sentences with the people who make films.

| actor    main character    director    ~~writer~~ |

**1** I'm the ¹ <u>writer</u> of the film – the script is all my work.

**2** I was in charge of how the film was made – I'm the ² _____.

**3** I'm a professional ³ _____ – I played the ⁴ _____ in this film.

**2** Write the nouns used to talk about films, next to the correct definitions.

| setting    ~~sequel~~    plot    special effects    acting    script |

**1** <u>sequel:</u> a film that follows on from an earlier film.
**2** _____: where a film takes place.
**3** _____: the written words the actors speak.
**4** _____: the story of a film.
**5** _____: special techniques used to make unusual scenes in films.
**6** _____: the way the actors perform in a film.

**3** Write the adjectives in the correct column of the table.

| ~~realistic~~    unoriginal    disappointing    extraordinary    unrealistic    original |

| Adjectives to say a film is good | Adjectives to say a film is bad |
|---|---|
| <u>realistic</u> | _____ |
| _____ | _____ |
| _____ | _____ |

## Use of English: verbs + –ing forms

SB p.10

**1** Look and match.

1 suggest      **a** to tell someone what you think they should do

2 avoid      **b** to say that you are happy with all the choices

3 not mind      **c** to choose not to do something

**2** Write sentences.

1 We / not mind / stay / here / for now.
   _We do not mind staying here for now._

2 She / avoid / play / basketball / yesterday.

   _____

3 He / suggest / go / to the cinema.

   _____

## Use of English: revision of present tenses

SB p.11

**Complete the sentences with the present simple or the present continuous.**

**1** The Earth _____ (rotate) on its axis once every 24 hours and _____ (move) once around the sun about every 365 days.

**2** Global temperatures _____ (go) up and sea levels _____ (rise).

**3** _____ (the director / make) a sequel at the moment?

**4** Water _____ (boil) at 100°C and _____ (freeze) at 0°C.

**5** _____ (you / usually read) film reviews?

**6** The cost of living _____ (increase) and salaries _____ (decrease).

## Speaking: making plans

SB p.12

**Choose the best sentences on page 8 to complete the conversation.**

**Sarah:** Let's get together next week.

**Maria:** ¹ _____ C _____

**Sarah:** Sorry, I have plans on Tuesday.

**Maria:** ² _____

**Sarah:** I don't have anything planned for Wednesday.

**Maria:** ³ _____

**Sarah:** That would be fun!

**Maria:** ⁴ _____

**Sarah:** I don't really like documentaries.

**Maria:** ⁵ _____

**Sarah:** Sounds good! I'll call you later and we can make a plan.

**A** What are you doing on Wednesday?    **B** Me too. I like films.

**C** Good idea! Are you busy on Tuesday?    **D** I prefer watching comedies to sci-fi.

**E** Oh, OK. How about watching a comedy?    **F** Shall we go to the cinema?

**G** Let's watch that new documentary.

## Use of English: revision of future forms

SB p.13

**1** Read and circle the correct option.

---

Dear Grandma,

I'm writing to tell you all my exciting plans. Tomorrow, I ¹_____ to the cinema with Lucy to watch a science-fiction film. It's all about what life ²_____ like in the future. I think it ³_____ brilliant! The film ⁴_____ at 5 o'clock, and then after the film we ⁵_____ dinner with Lucy's parents in a restaurant in town.

I hope you have a good time on holiday next week. ⁶_____ me some photographs? I ⁷_____ to show Mum this time!

⁸_____ on Sunday to say goodbye? Let me know what time is good for you.

Love,

Sarah

---

**1 a** will go    **b** go    (**c** 'm going to go)    **d** 's going to go

**2 a** is    **b** be    **c** will be    **d** is being

**3 a** is    **b** will be    **c** be    **d** won't be

**4 a** is beginning    **b** begins    **c** are going to begin    **d** begin

**5 a** 'm having    **b** 's having    **c** 're having    **d** will having

**6 a** You send    **b** Will you send    **c** Are you sending    **d** Do you send

**7 a** won't forget    **b** am not forgetting    **c** don't forget    **d** forget

**8 a** I call you    **b** Am I going to call you    **c** Shall I call you    **d** Am I calling you

## Focus on Drama

SB pp.14–15

**1** Number the stages of the scene in the correct order.

  ☐ Colin sees the lines on the wall.

  ☐ Pixie finds Richard's diary.

  ☐ 1 The children arrive at the house.

  ☐ They talk about the paintings.

  ☐ They find the door and go through it.

  ☐ Lightning lights up the door on the wall.

**2** **Read and complete.**

> stage directions        scenes        list of characters        act

This is the script for my new play. There's a ¹_____, which tells you who is in the play. I'm playing the part of Mark. I'm in all the ²_____ in the first ³_____, but I'm not in the second half of the play at all! There are useful ⁴_____, which tell us how to act the play.

**3** **Write the words next to the correct definitions.**

> brave   ~~frightened~~   silly   joking   wonder   shy   nervous   confident

1 _frightened_   :   afraid
2 _____   :   willing to do things that are dangerous without showing fear
3 _____   :   a feeling of great surprise or admiration
4 _____   :   worried about talking to people you don't know well
5 _____   :   worried about something
6 _____   :   feeling sure of your abilities and ideas
7 _____   :   something said in a way to make you laugh
8 _____   :   not behaving in a sensible way

*Check your progress*

1 **What can you do now?**

I can …

read and write film reviews ☐

use verbs + –ing forms ☐

understand and use phrases for making plans ☐

use a mixture of present and future forms ☐

act out and write a scene from a play ☐

**My learning**

What did you learn in this unit?

2 **Answer the questions about this unit.**

1 What have you enjoyed most?

_____

2 Is there anything you have found difficult?

_____

3 What would you like to learn more about?

_____

## Reading: understanding the text

SB p.19

**1** Look again at the text. Where do you think you are most likely to see a questionnaire like this?

  **a** in a leaflet giving information about a sports club

  **b** in a sports magazine

  **c** in a book about a famous person who plays sports

**2** Read and match the questions from the Student's Book. Complete the sentences.

  **1** Question 1 is about …

  **2** Questions 2 and 3 are about …

  **3** Question 4 is about …

  **a** what really matters in sport.

  **b** respecting adults who are in charge of the game.

  **c** behaving well whether you win or lose.

**3** Look at the answers that you gave in Activity 2 of the Student's Book and answer these questions.

  **1** Why do the **a** answers make you think that this person isn't a good sport?

  _____

  **2** Why do the **b** answers make you think that this person is trying to be a good sport?

  _____

  **3** Why do the **c** answers make you think that this person is a good sport?

  _____

## Reading: thinking about the text

SB p.19

**Answer the questions.**

**1** Why should we respect the referee and the coach?

_____

**2** Why do you think we should behave well whether we win or lose?

_____

**3** What do you think is the most important thing about playing sport and why?

_____

## Vocabulary: sports verbs

SB p.20

**Match the words with their meanings.**

| congratulate | respect | ~~celebrate~~ | sulk | cheat | argue |

**1** mark a happy event _celebrate_

**2** do something that is not honest because you want to get something _____

**3** have a good opinion of someone _____

**4** be silent for a while because you're angry about something _____

**5** express pleasure that something good has happened to someone _____

**6** disagree with someone about something _____

## Use of English: comparing using adverbs

SB p.20

**1** **Read and tick the correct sentence.**

**1** Henri finishes the walk in 32 minutes. Karl finishes the walk in 1 hour 14 minutes. Thomas finishes the walk in 1 hour 48 minutes.

  **a** Henri walks much faster than Karl. ☐

  **b** Henri walks just as fast as Karl. ☐

  **c** Thomas walks the fastest. ☐

**2** A cheetah can run 120 km/hour. A tiger can run 65 km/hour. An average house cat can run about 45 km/hour.

  **a** A tiger can't run as fast as a house cat. ☐

  **b** A tiger can run much faster than a cheetah. ☐

  **c** A cheetah runs the fastest. ☐

**2** **Complete the second sentence in each pair to mean the same as the first. Use the words _just as_, _slightly_, _much_ and _as_.**

**1** Laura played the game in 32 minutes. Hannah played the game in 41 minutes.
Laura played the game **much faster than** Hannah.

**2** Fran finished the bike race in 1 hour 13 minutes. Anna finished the bike race in 1 hour 14 minutes.

Fran cycled _____ Anna.

**3** Peta ran 14 km/hour and Chris ran 14 km/hour.

Peta ran _____ Chris.

**4** Calan types 30 words a minute and Luca types 10 words a minute.

Luca doesn't _____ Calan.

Review the meanings of the italic words in the questions. Use them in your answers.

**1** What's your greatest sporting *achievement*?

_____

**2** Have you ever won a *medal*? What colour and for what sport?

_____

_____

**3** Who is your favourite *professional athlete* and why?

_____

_____

**4** Which sports team do you *admire* most and why?

_____

**5** Have you ever done a *triathlon*? Would you like to? Why? / Why not?

_____


## Vocabulary: sports adjectives     SB p.22

**1** Write in the missing letters to make five sporting adjectives.

   **1** c _ mp _ titi _ e: wanting to be more successful than other people

   **2** s _ ro _ g: healthy, with good muscles

   **3** un _ it: not healthy or strong

   **4** h _ rd-w _ rkin _ : doing something seriously with a lot of effort

   **5** l _ z _ : not wanting to work

**2** Complete the sentences with adjectives from Activity 1 and explain your choices.

   **1** I would describe myself as _____ because _____

   _____.

   **2** I wouldn't describe myself as _____ because _____

   _____.

**1** **Choose the correct option.**

I ¹_____ a professional athlete for six years now. My greatest sporting achievement ²_____ when I won a gold medal in the triathlon at the Olympics. I thought the swimming was the hardest part of the race. While I ³_____, my leg suddenly ⁴_____ to hurt.

I thought the race was over for me, but I ⁵_____ going and I came first!

When I was young, I ⁶_____ about winning a gold medal, so dreams can come true!

| | | | |
|---|---|---|---|
| **1 a** was | **b** have been | **c** was being | **d** used to be |
| **2 a** was | **b** have been | **c** was being | **d** used to be |
| **3 a** swam | **b** have swum | **c** was swimming | **d** used to swim |
| **4 a** started | **b** has started | **c** was starting | **d** used to start |
| **5 a** kept | **b** have kept | **c** was keeping | **d** used to keep |
| **6 a** dream | **b** have dreamed | **c** was dreaming | **d** used to dream |

**2** **Complete the sentences with the correct form of the verb in brackets.**

1 This athlete _____ (win) a lot of medals so far this year.

2 When I was a little boy, I _____ (play) football every day after school before I hurt my knee.

3 He _____ (ride) his bicycle when he saw me.

4 My team and I _____ (celebrate) our win last week.

5 The player _____ (argue) with the referee when I arrived.

**Complete the sentences with the past perfect form of the verbs in brackets.**

1 When we arrived at the sports stadium, the match _____ (start).

2 After we _____ (finish) our practice, we played a real game.

3 Sarah _____ (read) a lot about running before she did a marathon.

4 Jamie couldn't play football for two months after he _____ (break) his arm.

5 When we got to the swimming pool, the race _____ (begin).

6 Martina _____ (warm up) before she took part in the race.

---

### Check your progress

**1 What can you do now?**

I can ...

complete and think about a questionnaire about being a good sport ☐

use a mixture of past tenses ☐

compare things using adverbs ☐

talk and write a fact file about an athlete I admire ☐

understand a text about where sports were first played ☐

carry out a sports survey ☐

**💡 My learning**
**What did you learn in this unit?**

**2 Answer the questions about this unit.**

1 What have you enjoyed most?

_____

2 Is there anything you have found difficult?

_____

3 What would you like to learn more about?

_____

# 3  School rules!

## Reading: comprehension

SB p.30

**1** Read the article again. Read the sentences and write *true* or *false*. Correct any sentences that are false.

**1** Some children can't go to school because they live too far away from their nearest school. _____

**2** Some children in Bangladesh go to school on boats. _____

**3** There is no school equipment on the school boats in Bangladesh. _____

**4** Some children in Bangladesh go to school in Solar-Powered Internet Schools. _____

**5** The children who talk about their travelling schools like them. _____

**2** Complete the sentences.

The schools in the article are:

**1** different to my school because _____.

**2** similar to my school because _____.

## Reading: scanning for specific information

SB p.30

Scan the text and answer these questions in two minutes. Time yourself!

**1** What's the name of the student from South Africa? _____Lefa_____

**2** Is the Solar-Powered Internet School made of metal or wood? _____

**3** Where does Kakoli come from? _____

**4** Where did the first Solar-Powered Internet School open? _____

**5** What does Kakoli want to be when she grows up? _____

## Reading: thinking about the text

SB p.30

Think of questions that you would like to ask Kakoli and Lefa and then swap with a partner. Write answers you think Kakoli and Lefa might give.

**Kakoli:**

Question: _____?

Answer: _____.

**Lefa:**

Question: _____?

Answer: _____.

## Vocabulary: words in context

**1** Complete the dictionary entries with the words from the box.

> tablet    laptop    printer    whiteboard

**1** _____ (noun)
*a machine that prints*

**2** _____ (noun)
*where a teacher shows information in a classroom*

**3** _____ (noun)
*a small, thin computer*

**4** _____ (noun)
**a** *a small, thin computer with a touchscreen*
**b** *a medicine that you eat*

**2** Look and write words from Activity 1.

**1** I like to do language activities on a _____ .

**2** I write my essays on a _____ .

**3** Our teacher writes new words on the _____ .

**4** I only use the _____ when I have to because I want to save paper.

**3** Complete the text.

> solar-powered    energy    canal    opportunity

When you visit Amsterdam, don't miss out on the ¹ _____ of taking a boat trip on the ² _____ . There are even some ³ _____ boats, which run on clean ⁴ _____ .

# Use of English: present perfect

SB p.32

**1** **Write sentences using the present perfect.**

**1** Sarah can't find her homework. She / lose / it. _____She has lost it_____

**2** Marco fell over. But / he / not hurt himself. _____

**3** There's no juice in the fridge. Anita / drink / it. _____

**4** The children aren't here. They / go out. _____

**5** There's some cake left. Nadia and Ayesha / not finish / it. _____

**2** **Read and match.**

**1** I have *just* eaten an ice cream.

**2** I haven't eaten an ice cream *yet*.

**3** Have you *ever* eaten an ice cream?

**4** I have *never* eaten an ice cream.

**a** I don't know what ice cream is like. I haven't eaten it *at any time in my life up to now*.

**b** I finished eating an ice cream *a short time ago*.

**c** There's an ice cream in the freezer. I didn't eat it *at any time up to now*.

**d** Have you eaten an ice cream *at any time in your life up to now*?

**3** **Read and complete the sentences, using the present perfect and one of the time adverbs from Activity 2.**

**1** Your friend thinks you have finished your dinner and takes your plate.

You say: Wait a minute, I _haven't finished yet_ (not / finish).

**2** You drink a big glass of water. Your mother asks, 'Are you thirsty?'

You reply: No, I _____
(have) a glass of water.

**3** Your friend has been skateboarding for the first time. She wants to know about you.

She asks: _____
(you / be) skateboarding?

**4** You haven't been skateboarding.

You tell your friend: No, I _____
(try) skateboarding.

Complete the country names and write the continents.

Africa　　Asia (×4)　　North America

| Country | Continent |
|---|---|
| **1** S<u>ou</u>th Af<u>ri</u>ca | Africa |
| **2** B_ng_ad_s_ | |
| **3** I_don_si_ | |
| **4** C_in_ | |
| **5** U_it_d　_tat_s　o_　Am_ri_a | |
| **6** _ndi_ | |

**1** **Unscramble and rewrite the sentences.**

**1** is / for / Waiting / train / boring / a

_____

**2** really / Daniel / swimming / loves

_____

**3** instrument / fun / Learning / is / a / musical

_____

**4** stopping / drove / school / We / to / without

_____

**5** meeting / friends / her / really / enjoyed / She

_____

**2** **Write three sentences of your own, using the _–ing_ form as a noun.**

**1** _____

_____

**2** _____

_____

**3** _____

_____

**Choose the correct options.**

1 I love my school and learning new things. I think that our most important human right is the right to [**property / education / speech**].

2 I've just bought my first house. I think the right to own [**assembly / property / education**] is one of the most basic human rights.

3 I've got a lot of opinions about current affairs! For me, the most important human right is freedom of [**speech / property / education**].

4 I think that every human being has the right to be [**free / private / basic**], unless you break the law.

5 I love meeting up with my friends in a group. I didn't realise that this is our right to [**education / speech / assembly**] until my mum told me!

6 I think that actors have a right to a [**free / private / fair**] life. We don't need to know every detail of what they do.

---

### Check your progress

**My learning**
What did you learn in this unit?

1 **What can you do now?**

I can …

understand the main points and specific information in a text ☐

use the present perfect ☐

understand the main points and specific information in a podcast ☐

plan and write about my opinion about schools ☐

design a perfect school ☐

understand and talk about human rights ☐

2 **Answer the questions about this unit.**

1 What have you enjoyed most?

_____

2 Is there anything you have found difficult?

_____

3 What would you like to learn more about?

_____

# 4 Bookworms

## Listening: vocabulary

SB p.40

**Read and complete.**

connection    habits    ~~interview~~    literature    professor    report

Tomorrow, I've got an [1] <u>interview</u> at the university with a [2] _____ of American [3] _____. He wrote a [4] _____, which shows a [5] _____ between parents' and children's reading [6] _____.

## Use of English: questions with prepositions

SB p.42

**1** Choose the correct options.

1 [**In / On**] which magazine did you read this article?

2 [**On / At**] what time does the library open?

3 What day were you born [**on / in**]?

4 Which country do you come [**at / from**]?

5 Who does this book belong [**to / for**]?

6 [**In / On**] which author are you interested?

**2** Complete the questions with the correct prepositions.

in    at    to    by    ~~from~~    of    for    on

1 <u>From</u> whose point of view is the story told?

2 _____ what time does the reading group begin?

3 _____ which direction is the library?

4 Which book is she the author _____ ?

5 Which book group do you belong _____?

6 What reason was this book written _____?

7 _____ what date was the author born?

8 _____ what name is the author best known?

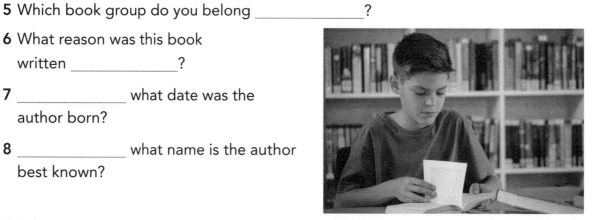

## Reading: comprehension

SB p.43

**1** **Read and circle.**

**1** There [are / aren't] enough libraries for all the people living in Bogota.

**2** The libraries [are / aren't] in the areas where poor people live.

**3** Gutierrez has made a library [but he doesn't like reading / and he loves reading].

**4** Gutierrez's [father / mother] loved reading, too.

**5** Gutierrez thinks that books are better than [films / e-readers].

**2** **Read the text again and answer the questions.**

**1** Where does Gutierrez live? _____

**2** How many years has he worked as a rubbish collector? _____

**3** How many books has he collected? _____

**4** How many people live in Bogota? _____

**5** How many libraries are there? _____

**6** Who are Gutierrez's favourite authors? _____

## Reading: thinking about the text

SB p.43

**Write three questions of your own about the text. Swap with a partner and answer.**

**1** Question: _____  Answer: _____

**2** Question: _____  Answer: _____

**3** Question: _____  Answer: _____

## Vocabulary: words in context

SB p.44

**Complete the sentences with words from the box.**

| invention | community | rescued | luxuries | rubbish |
| afford | e-books | e-reader | | |

**1** We can't really _____ to buy _____.

**2** How many _____ do you have on your _____?

**3** The _____ has come together to clear up the _____ on the beach.

**4** The inventor _____ his latest _____ from the fire.

## Reading: newspaper articles

**1** Write the headlines in full sentences. Use the present perfect.

**1** RUBBISH COLLECTOR RESCUES BOOKS FOR COLOMBIAN CHILDREN

_A rubbish collector has rescued some books for some Colombian children._

**2** SCIENTISTS DISCOVER TOO MUCH SCREEN TIME BAD FOR CHILDREN

_____

_____

**3** FLOODS DESTROY OVER 500 HOMES

_____

**2** Complete the text with words from the box.

> articles    simple    rules    verbs    perfect    sentences

- Headlines do not follow the normal ¹ _____ of English grammar because they are not written in full ² _____.

- They don't usually include ³ _____ (for example, 'a' or 'the').

- Sometimes, ⁴ _____ can be left out of a sentence – when these are used, ⁵ _____ tenses are more common than ⁶ _____ tenses.

**3** In your notebook, write the first paragraph of this article. Answer the five *Wh–* questions about the article. *Who? What? When? Why? Where?*

**FLOODS DESTROY OVER 500 HOMES**

## Use of English: connectives for contrast

Rewrite the pairs of sentences as one sentence using the connective in italics.

**1** Most of my friends like digital books. I prefer printed books.                    *while*

_Most of my friends like digital books, while I prefer printed books._

**2** The library is small. It has got a lot of books.                    *Although*

_____

**3** Sam goes to the library every day. It's a long way from his house.                    *though*

_____

_____

**4** Kelly likes fiction. Jane prefers non-fiction.                    *while*

_____

# Literature: what makes a good story?

**1** Match words and meanings.

1 hero
2 style
3 structure
4 truth
5 imagination

a the main character in a book
b the ability to think of a lot of ideas
c all the facts about something
d the way in which a story is organised
e the way a book is written

**2** Complete the diagram with words from the box.

style    characters    ~~ideas~~    structure

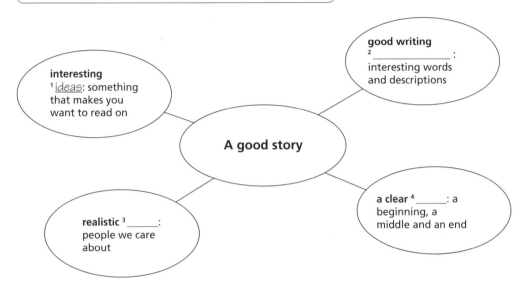

**interesting**
¹ _ideas_: something that makes you want to read on

**good writing**
² _____ : interesting words and descriptions

**A good story**

**realistic** ³ _____: people we care about

**a clear** ⁴ _____: a beginning, a middle and an end

**3** What things do you think make a story a good story and why? Use the ideas from the diagram and your own ideas.

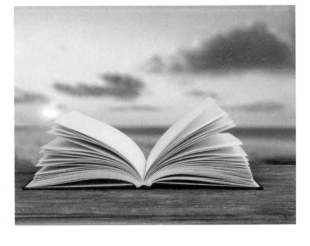

_____

_____

_____

_____

_____

_____

_____

_____

_____

_____

**1** **Find 12 types of books. Match with meanings.**

| t | r | a | v | e | l | a | g | z | d | l | f | g | w | d |
|---|---|---|---|---|---|---|---|---|---|---|---|---|---|---|
| x | y | z | y | b | q | u | e | s | p | o | r | t | s | v |
| v | p | m | k | j | r | t | j | c | x | y | s | a | a | q |
| j | y | c | b | u | o | o | e | i | w | t | q | f | m | k |
| e | w | h | v | i | m | b | k | e | a | w | h | m | r | v |
| b | p | k | a | w | a | i | c | n | b | o | q | h | t | q |
| r | d | e | i | h | n | o | o | c | n | a | t | r | o | l |
| e | i | g | f | i | c | g | m | e | a | d | h | q | p | d |
| u | o | m | c | s | e | r | e | f | q | v | o | l | w | f |
| i | r | r | t | t | a | a | d | i | n | e | r | v | d | c |
| t | z | b | m | o | n | p | y | c | g | n | r | o | k | y |
| i | g | g | v | r | k | h | m | t | q | t | o | y | i | e |
| z | r | k | e | y | f | y | h | i | l | u | r | e | a | e |
| i | k | x | u | u | i | b | i | o | g | r | a | p | h | y |
| o | i | p | x | j | p | v | m | n | m | e | i | q | r | z |

**FICTION**

**1** <u>romance</u>: a story about people who love each other

**2** _____ : a story that is very frightening

**3** _____ : a story about something unusual, exciting and perhaps dangerous

**4** _____ : a story about something funny

**5** _____ : a story about things that happen in the future or in other parts of the universe

**NON-FICTION**

**6** _____ : a story of the life of a person written by another person

**7** _____ : the story of your life that you write yourself

**8** _____ : a story about a journey to an interesting place

**9** _____ : a story about things that happened in the past

**10** _____ : a story about sportsmen or sportswomen

## Check your progress

**1 What can you do now?**

I can …

listen to and understand an interview ☐

use questions with prepositions ☐

use connectives for contrast ☐

talk and write about the advantages and disadvantages of e-readers ☐

understand and talk about literature ☐

**💡 My learning**
**What did you learn in this unit?**

**2 Answer the questions about this unit.**

**1** What have you enjoyed most?

_____

**2** Is there anything you have found difficult?

_____

**3** What would you like to learn more about?

_____

# 5 Extreme weather

## Vocabulary: extreme weather

SB p.52

Read and match.

| | | | |
|---|---|---|---|
| 1 a cold spell | | a | thick cloud that is close to the ground |
| 2 a heat wave | | b | a period of time with low temperatures |
| 3 fog | | c | a long period of time with no rain |
| 4 a drought | | d | when a lot of water covers an area that is usually dry |
| 5 a flood | | e | a period of time with high temperatures |
| 6 a hurricane | | f | a storm with very strong winds and rain |

## Use of English: present simple passive and past simple passive

SB p.53

**1** Complete the sentences using the passive form.

1 The thunderstorm _is expected_ (expect) to arrive later today.

2 The house _____ (not flood) at the moment.

3 _____ (people / advise) to stay indoors until the hurricane is over?

4 _____ (elderly people / warn) to take extra care in the heat wave last week.

5 _____ (A severe weather warning / not give) yesterday and it didn't snow.

6 _____ (you / wake up) last night by the storm?

**2** Complete the second sentence using the passive form.

1 Experts warn drivers only to travel if necessary.
  Drivers _are warned_ only to travel if necessary.

2 Weather forecasters don't expect snow today.

  Snow _____ today.

3 Doctors asked people to check on elderly neighbours during cold spells.

  People _____ to check.

4 Weather forecasters didn't predict the thick fog yesterday morning.

  Thick fog _____ yesterday morning.

5 Teachers advised parents with young children to take extra care during the heat wave.

  Parents with young children _____ to take extra care during the heat wave.

## Vocabulary: weather forecasts

**1** Read and write the points on the compass.

north    south    east    west    north-west
north-east    south-west    south-east

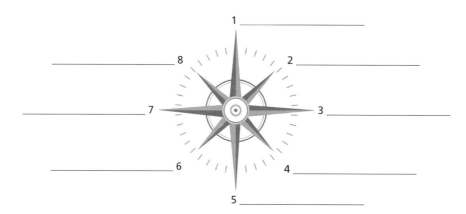

1 _____

8 _____    2 _____

7 _____    3 _____

6 _____    4 _____

5 _____

**2** Write the common phrases you will hear in weather forecasts in the correct column of the table below.

difficult / dangerous driving conditions

People are warned to expect …

A severe weather warning was given …

People are advised to …

The storm / fog is expected to clear by …

Allow extra time for journeys and only travel if necessary.

| Information about weather | General advice | Advice for drivers |
|---|---|---|
| 1 _____ _____ _____ | 3 _____ _____ _____ | 5 _____ _____ _____ |
| 2 _____ _____ _____ | 4 _____ _____ _____ | 6 _____ _____ _____ |

# Reading: comprehension

SB p.54

**1** Read the text and write true (T) or false (F). Correct any sentences that are false.

**1** The blogger was woken up by the storm just after midnight. _____

**2** He went outside into the garden to watch the storm. _____

**3** There was a lot of thunder and lightning. _____

**4** He didn't get wet. _____

**5** He felt sad when the storm finished. _____

**6** Everyone else was woken up by the storm as well. _____

**2** You want to tell your friend about the blog. Describe it in one or two sentences.

I read this interesting blog today. It was about …

_____

_____

# Use of English: adjectives with –*ing* and –*ed* endings

SB p.55

Complete the crossword by reading the clues and making adjectives from the verbs in the box.

amaze    terrify    exhaust    disappoint    shock

**Across**

**1** when you feel surprised in a good way

**2** when you feel surprised in a bad way

**5** something that makes you feel very tired

**6** when you feel sad because you didn't get what you had hoped for

**7** when you feel very frightened

**8** something that makes you feel very frightened

**9** something that makes you feel surprised in a bad way

**Down**

**1** something that surprises you in a good way

**3** when you feel very tired

**4** something that makes you feel sad because you didn't get what you had hoped for

## Use of English: *this, that, these* and *those* | SB p.55

**Choose the correct options.**

1 There were very strong winds last year. [That / Those] were the worst winds I had ever experienced.

2 There has been no rain for three months. [This / These] has caused a lot of problems for farmers.

3 [This / These] are the worst storms we've had in years.

4 It will be sunny today, but [that / those] will all change tomorrow when the rain moves in.

5 [This / These] is the longest drought this area has ever known.

6 There were several floods last year. [This / These] caused lots of problems for local residents.

## Writing: descriptions | SB p.56

**1** **Imagine that you are standing in the rain in a storm. Complete the sentences.**

1 I can see _____ .

2 I can hear _____ .

3 I can smell _____ .

4 I can feel _____ .

5 I can taste _____ .

**2** **Use your imagination to rewrite the sentences using similes.**

1 The wind was loud.

The wind was as loud as _____ .

2 The snow was soft.

The snow was as soft as _____ .

3 The sun was very hot.

The sun was as hot as _____ .

4 The lightning is bright.

The lightning is like _____ .

5 The storm is strong.

The storm is like _____ .

6 The rainfall was heavy.

The rainfall was like _____ .

**1** **Choose the correct options.**

Text messages are usually [1] [formal / informal]. They [2] [follow / don't follow] the usual rules of grammar and spelling. You [3] [have to / don't have to] use full sentences and you [4] [can / can't] use abbreviations – short ways of writing words. You [5] [have / don't have] to start or finish text messages in any particular way.

**2** **Write the text message abbreviations as full sentences.**

**1** C u 2mro. _____

**2** Lk 4wd 2 it. _____

**3** Spk l8tr _____

**4** How r u? _____

---

### Check your progress

**1 What can you do now?**

I can …

listen to and understand a weather forecast ☐

talk about extreme weather ☐

use present simple and past simple passive ☐

read a descriptive blog ☐

write a descriptive blog ☐

understand and talk about floods in geography ☐

**2 Answer the questions about this unit.**

**1** What have you enjoyed most?

_____

**2** Is there anything you have found difficult?

_____

**3** What would you like to learn more about?

_____

### 💡 My learning

What did you learn in this unit?

## Vocabulary: our planet

SB p.62

**1** Write the numbers from the map next to the correct words below.

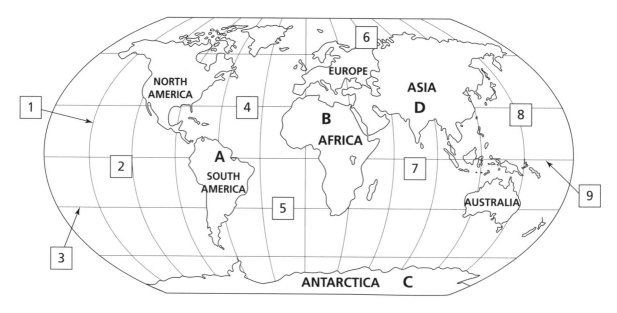

Pacific Ocean ☐   Atlantic Ocean ☐   line of longitude ☐

Pacific Ocean ☐   Atlantic Ocean ☐   line of latitude ☐

Arctic Ocean ☐   Equator ☐   Indian Ocean ☐

**2** Complete the sentences.

**1** The best place I've been is _____ because _____

_____.

**2** I want to visit _____ because _____

_____.

**3** I don't want to go to _____ because _____

_____.

## Reading: comprehension

SB p.63

**1** Read the text again and match the places to A–D on the map above.

| Mount Everest   River Nile   Amazon rainforest   Vostok Station |

**2 Read and match.**

| | |
|---|---|
| 1 Scientists think that the Earth is | a on 13 September 1922. |
| 2 Mount Everest is | b 6.5 million square kilometres. |
| 3 The River Nile is | |
| 4 The Amazon River is | c 6650 kilometres long. |
| 5 The Amazon rainforest is | d 4.54 billion years old. |
| 6 The Pacific Ocean is | e 155 million square kilometres. |
| 7 The hottest temperature on Earth was taken | f on 21 July 1983. |
| | g 6400 kilometres long. |
| 8 The coldest temperature on Earth was taken | h 8848 metres high. |

**3 Research these questions. Where did you find the answers? Use sources you can trust!**

1 Who was the first woman to climb Mount Everest?
2 Which countries does the Amazon River go through?
3 Approximately, how many plant species live in the Amazon rainforest?
4 What's the largest island in the Pacific Ocean?

**4 Complete the sentences.**

1 The most interesting thing I learned about the Earth today is _____

2 The most surprising thing I learned about the Earth today is _____

3 I would like to find out more about _____ because _____

## Vocabulary: extreme adjectives

SB p.64

**1 Rewrite the sentences replacing the words in bold with an extreme adjective.**
1 The mountain in front of us was **very big**.

_____

2 The food we ate in Vietnam was **extremely good**.

_____

3 Sarah's suitcase is **extremely big**!

_____

4 The weather during the journey was **very good**.

_____

**2 Write two sentences of your own using extreme adjectives.**

1 _____

2 _____

## Vocabulary: words in context

SB p.64

Complete the words.

1 v_l_an_

2 o_e_n

3 p_ak

4 p_pu_at_o_

5 r_i_f_re_t

6 r_c_s

## Use of English: adding information with *which, who* and *where*

SB p.65

Complete the text with *which, who* or *where.*

A desert is an extremely dry area, ¹_____ there is less than 250 mm of rain a year. The driest place in the world is the Atacama Desert, ²_____ is in Chile and Peru. At its centre is a place that scientists call absolute desert, ³_____ rain has never been recorded. It may be surprising to find out that the Atacama has a population of more than a million people, ⁴_____ mostly live in the cities near the sea. There are also some farmers, ⁵_____ grow olives, tomatoes and cucumbers, in the far north. The night skies, ⁶_____ are usually completely clear, make the Atacama Desert one of the best places in the world to look at the stars.

## Use of English: adding information with *whose*

SB p.65

**1** Look again at this sentence from the text in the Student's Book and choose the correct options.

*This Antarctic station, **whose** winter population is only 13 scientists and engineers, reached a temperature low of −89.2 °C on 21 July 1983.*

The word [1][whose / who's] is used in relative clauses to show possession. It replaces the words [2][he, she, it or they / him, her, it or them / his, her, its or their].

**Spelling tip**

Don't confuse the relative pronoun *whose* with *who's* (who is). They sound the same, but the spelling is different.

**2** Write one sentence instead of two using a relative clause.

**1** Edmund Hillary climbed Mount Everest in 1953. His guide was called Tenzing Norgay.

   <u>Edmund Hillary, whose guide was called Tenzing Norgay, climbed Mount Everest in 1953.</u>

**2** The people of the Amazon rainforest have lived there for thousands of years. Their homes are in danger.

_____

**3** The scientists in Antarctica live in difficult conditions. Their work is very important.

_____

## Vocabulary: useful verbs

SB p.66

**1** Replace the underlined phrases in the sentences with the correct form of the verbs from the box.

> disappear    hunt    recycle    destroy

**1** Snakes are being <u>chased and killed</u> for their skin.
**2** Many of the monkeys' habitats have <u>gone away</u>.
**3** The rainforest is being <u>damaged</u> by tourism.
**4** It's important that we <u>use</u> paper <u>again</u>.

# Use of English: present continuous passive

Rewrite the sentences in the passive. Only use *by* if we need to know who did the action of the verb.

**1** Something is destroying these bees' habitats.

*These bees' habitats are being destroyed.*

**2** People aren't hunting elephants in this area.

_____

**3** The snake is hunting the mouse.

_____

**4** People are recycling a lot of paper in this town.

_____

**5** Are humans hurting the environment?

_____

---

*Check your progress*

1 **What can you do now?**

I can …

    read and talk about extreme places  ☐

    use non-defining relative clauses  ☐

    listen to and think about a presentation about extreme animals  ☐

    talk about and write about my opinion  ☐

    read an article about an extreme world tour and plan a trip  ☐

2 **Answer the questions about this unit.**

  **1** What have you enjoyed most?

  _____

  **2** Is there anything you have found difficult?

  _____

  **3** What would you like to learn more about?

  _____

*My learning*
What did you learn in this unit?

# 7 Back in time

## Vocabulary: talking about history

SB p.74

**1** Look and write.

| knight | tomb | mummy | battle |

**1**

**2**

**3**

**4**

_____  _____  _____  _____

**2** Choose the correct options.

I went to a brilliant ¹[**exhibition / expedition**] at the museum last weekend. It was all about what life was like during the Middle ²[**Years / Ages**]. I think this ³[**period / length**] of history is more interesting than ⁴[**antique / ancient**] history.

There was a ⁵[**virtual / practical**] reality show, which showed us what people's homes were really like. Who needs to visit real historical ⁶[**sites / scenes**] when you can see everything in the museum!

**3** Complete the sentences.

**1** My favourite period of history is _____ because _____.

**2** If I had a time machine, I would go back to _____
because _____.

## Reading: comprehension

SB p.75

**Read the texts again. Write *True* or *False* or *Doesn't say*.**

**1** Mark went to an exhibition about the Middle Ages. _____

**2** Mark learned about King Tutankhamun. _____

**3** Tim got a virtual reality app about history for his birthday. _____

**4** Tim's app tells you about the famous people who were alive during the Great Fire of London. _____

**5** Jan comes from the USA. _____

**6** Jan went to visit a historical site last week. _____

## Reading: research

SB p.75

**Find answers to these questions. Give your sources. Use only sources that you trust!**

1 *I want to find out more about Ancient Egypt now. I wonder what sort of people were made into mummies …*

_____

_____

_____

Source: _____

2 *Now, I want to find out more about it, for example, how did the Great Fire of London start?*

_____

_____

_____

Source: _____

3 *I wonder what it was like to be a knight in the Middle Ages …*

_____

_____

_____

Source: _____

## Use of English: more compound nouns

SB p.76

**1** **Use one word from each box to make six compound nouns.**

| country̶ back sun | | mother house si̶d̶e̶ |
| guide step farm | | book shine ground |

1 *countryside*

2 _____

3 _____

4 _____

5 _____

6 _____

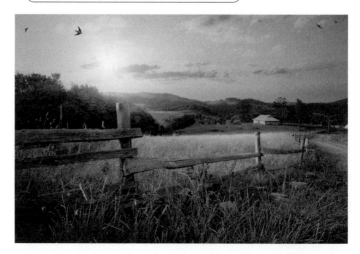

**2** Complete the text with the compound nouns from Activity 1.

Yesterday, I had a lovely day out in the ¹ <u>countryside</u> with my ² _____.
We visited an old ³ _____ and gardens. We bought an interesting
⁴ _____, which told us all about the historical ⁵ _____ of
the house. After we had explored the house, we went for a long walk in the
⁶ _____.

## Use of English: past perfect with *never, ever, always* and *already*

SB p.78

**1** Circle the correct option to complete the sentences.

**1** I had [**ever** / **never**] visited such an interesting museum before.

**2** Had you [**ever** / **always**] studied Egyptian history before you moved to this school?

**3** The play had [**already** / **always**] started by the time they arrived.

**4** Sara had [**ever** / **always**] wanted to visit London.

**5** The archaeologist had [**always** / **never**] been inside a tomb before.

**6** The students had [**already** / **always**] finished the exam when the bell rang.

**7** We had [**already** / **never**] seen so many visitors at an exhibition before.

**8** The history teacher had [**already** / **ever**] taught the students about the Middle Ages.

**2** Put the phrases in the correct order to write the sentences.

**1** had already opened / by the time / The exhibition / we arrived

_____

**2** before you studied / visited a castle / the Middle Ages / Had you ever / ?

_____

**3** history books / Mark / reading / had always enjoyed

_____

**4** a film about / We / before / had never seen / the Great Fire of London

_____

**5** to visit / The students / wanted / Egypt / had always

_____

**6** before / Sarah and Dan / worn / virtual reality headsets / had never

_____

**7** to the United States? / worked / Had Jane ever / she came / in a museum / before

_____

**8** had always / at university / Ella / wanted / to study history

_____

**3** Complete the sentences with the correct form of the verbs from the box.

> never / see     never / listen to     you / ever / try
> Peter / ever / read     already / hear     ~~always / think~~

**1** We <u>had always thought</u> that King Tutankhamun was just a character in a story.

**2** They _____ a real mummy until they went to the exhibition last month.

**3** _____ a virtual reality headset before you went to the exhibition?

**4** By the time the archaeologist arrived at the site, he _____ the news.

**5** The students _____ a lecture about the Middle Ages before.

**6** _____ a book about the Great Fire of London before he studied it at school?

## Focus on History: archaeologists' greatest finds

SB pp.80–81

**1** Read and match.

**1** How long was Howard Carter looking for King Tutankhamun's tomb?

**2** In what year did Howard Carter find King Tutankhamun's tomb?

**3** In what year did King Tutankhamun die?

**4** In what year were the ruins of Pompeii found?

**5** In what year did a volcano bury the city of Pompeii?

**6** How long was Pompeii under the rock?

**7** In what year was the Terracotta Army found?

**8** In what year was the Terracotta Army made?

**9** In what year were the bones of King Richard III found?

**10** In what year did King Richard III die?

**a** c1346 BCE

**b** 2000 years

**c** 1485

**d** 1922

**e** 209 BCE

**f** 2013

**g** 31 years

**h** 1748

**i** 79 CE

**j** 1974

**2** Complete the sentences.

**1** I think that the work done by archaeologists is _____

because _____.

**2** I would / wouldn't like to be an archaeologist because _____.

# Vocabulary: useful words for talking about history

Complete the crossword.

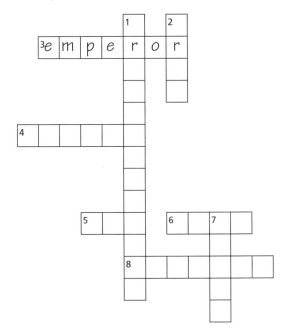

## Across

**3** a man who rules a group of countries

**4** a large model of a person or animal, made of stone or metal

**5** to make a hole in the ground

**6** to put something in a hole in the ground and cover it up

**8** a person in an army

## Down

**1** a person whose job is to look for and study old things

**2** a large group of soldiers who are trained to fight battles on land

**7** the parts of a building that remain after something destroys the rest

---

*Check your progress*

**1 What can you do now?**

I can …

read and talk about historical experiences ☐

use the past perfect ☐

listen to and think about famous people from the past ☐

read and talk about the work of archaeologists ☐

make a time capsule ☐

**2 Answer the questions about this unit.**

1 What have you enjoyed most?

_____

2 Is there anything you have found difficult?

_____

3 What would you like to learn more about?

_____

*My learning*
What did you learn in this unit?

## Vocabulary: identity and character

SB p.84

**1** Match the adjectives to the descriptions.

> warm    calm    generous    confident    independent    creative

**1** I like drawing and painting. I also write my own poems and songs.

_____

**2** I am happy to do things on my own and don't need help from others.

_____

**3** I give as much money as I can to charity and sometimes I give up my time to clean up rubbish at the beach near my house.

_____

**4** People say that I'm very friendly.

_____

**5** I'm not shy because I'm sure about my own abilities and ideas.

_____

**6** When things get hard, I don't get worried or angry or excited.

_____

**2** Choose the correct options to complete the sentences.

**1** I have a strong sense of my own _____. I know who I am.
   **a** identity        **b** quality        **c** specification

**2** What _____ do you identify with, male, female or neither?
   **a** role        **b** person        **c** gender

**3** I'm half French and half Italian, so I have two _____!
   **a** places        **b** nationalities        **c** locations

**4** I want to work in the _____, perhaps for a newspaper, or in TV or radio.
   **a** media        **b** medium        **c** social media

**5** My sister has a different _____ to me but we're good friends!
   **a** person        **b** character        **c** quality

## Reading: comprehension

SB p.85

Read the texts again and complete the sentences.

1 Marco grew up in _____ and is proud to be _____.

2 Saira's view is that men often aren't as _____ as women and that women often aren't as _____ as men.

3 Lucien's mum is _____ and his dad is _____.

4 Every day, Arjun reads the _____ on the internet.

5 Kalifa's friends have helped her to feel more _____ at school.

## Reading: thinking about the text

SB p.85

1 Which of the people on page 85 of the Student's Book are most similar to you and why?

_____

_____

2 Write your own post to add to the chat room. Talk about who you are and what's important in making your identity.

_____

_____

_____

_____

## Writing: spelling patterns

SB p.86

Correct the spelling mistake in each sentence.

1 I'm not very ~~confidant~~ and feel shy when I meet new people.
  *confident*

2 Jin is always keen on having new experiances.


3 My brother is very generus and always helps me when he can.


4 The students are independunt and work well on their own.


5 There are a lot of differeses between me and my sister.


6 Sport is an enormouss part of my identity.

## Use of English: adjectives + prepositions

SB p.86

**1** **Read and match.**

1 proud of       a worried

2 amazed at       b the same in some ways but not every way

3 keen on/fond of       c pleased about something good that you or other people close to you have done

4 similar to       d surprised

5 anxious about       e like something very much

**2** **Complete each sentence with an adjective and preposition from Activity 1.**

1 I'm very ___fond of___ going to the cinema. I try to go every week.

2 I feel very _____ _____ my exams. I hope that I do well.

3 I look very _____ _____ my brother. We both have brown eyes and hair.

4 I'm very _____ _____ the goal that I scored today!

5 I was _____ _____ today's news. It was a real surprise.

6 I'm not very _____ _____ fish. I prefer eating meat and vegetables.

**3** **Complete the sentences with your own ideas.**

1 I'm very proud of _____.

2 I sometimes feel anxious about _____.

3 I'm very fond of _____.

4 I'm similar to _____.

## Use of English: reported speech

SB p.88

**1** **Complete the sentences in reported speech. Remember only to change the tense if you need to.**

1 Lucia said, 'I don't like going to the cinema.'

Lucia said that _she doesn't like going to the cinema._

2 'These are the books I read on holiday,' said Adam to his sister.

Adam told his sister that _____

3 'We're travelling to Beijing tomorrow,' said Sophia.

Sophia said that _____

4 Aisha said, 'this is where we stayed yesterday.'

Aisha said that _____

5 Robert said, 'I have never been to this restaurant.'

Robert said that _____

**2** **Read the conversation. Then complete the text below.**

**Reema:** Hey, Rachel, [1] **I'm talking** to you from the top of the Eiffel Tower.

**Rachel:** Really?! Lucky you! [2] **I'm** at college [3] **today**!

**Reema:** Oh sorry! [4] **We arrived** in Paris [5] **yesterday** and [6] **we're staying** in a lovely hotel [7] **here**. I [8] **haven't been** to France since [9] **last year** and [10] **I'm** happy to be back!

Reema said that [1] _she was talking_ to Rachel from the top of the Eiffel Tower. Rachel

said that [2] _____ at college [3] _____. Reema said

that [4] _____ in Paris [5] _____ and that [6] _____

in a lovely hotel [7] _____. She said that [8] _____ to France

since [9] _____ and that [10] _____ happy to be back.

## Focus on Literature: non-fiction

SB pp.90–91

**1** **Match the verbs from the text to the meanings.**

| | |
|---|---|
| **1** copy | **a** not stop |
| **2** pick | **b** try to do what another person does |
| **3** continue | **c** choose |
| **4** promise | **d** form a picture of something in your mind |
| **5** pronounce | **e** say that you will certainly do something |
| **6** imagine | **f** make the sound of a word |

**2** Look again at the text and write *True* or *False*.

**1** Caitlin had visited Zimbabwe before she started writing to Martin. _____

**2** Caitlin was 12 years old when she started writing to Martin. _____

**3** In her first letter, Caitlin told Martin about her hobbies. _____

**4** There was a letter for every pupil in Martin's class. _____

**5** Martin told Caitlin that he enjoyed playing soccer. _____

**6** Martin wasn't sure if he was going to carry on writing to Caitlin. _____

**3** Complete the sentences.

**1** I (enjoy / don't enjoy) reading non-fiction books because _____

_____

_____

**2** I (enjoyed / didn't enjoy) the extracts from *I Will Always Write Back* because

_____

_____

_____

---

**Check your progress**

**1 What can you do now?**

I can …

read and talk about what's important for personal identity ☐

use adjectives ☐

use prepositions and reported speech ☐

understand speakers' opinions ☐

check what somebody has said ☐

write an email about myself ☐

**My learning**

What did you learn in this unit?

**2 Answer the questions about this unit.**

**1** What have you enjoyed most?

_____

**2** Is there anything you have found difficult?

_____

**3** What would you like to learn more about?

_____

# Mid-year review

## Vocabulary: word hunt

**Name four …**

1 types of films _____ _____ _____ _____

2 people who work in sports _____ _____ _____ _____

3 countries or continents _____ _____ _____ _____

4 types of books _____ _____ _____ _____

5 types of weather _____ _____ _____ _____

6 ways to describe feelings _____ _____ _____ _____

7 interesting natural features _____ _____ _____ _____

8 ways to describe people's character _____ _____ _____ _____

## Vocabulary: a crossword puzzle

**Complete the crossword.**

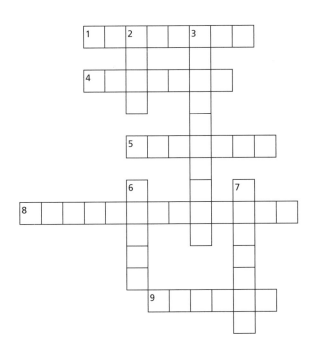

**Across**

1 the person who is against you in a sports competition

4 a long period of time with no rain

5 the environment in which an animal or a plant lives or grows

8 person who studies items from the past, for example, buildings and tools

9 a book or film that is very frightening

**Down**

2 the story of a film or book

3 a public event where art or interesting objects are shown

6 small metal disc (usually gold, silver or bronze) you get for doing something good

7 books about people and events that are not real

## Writing: punctuation

**Read and correct the punctuation in the short story. There are seven missing punctuation marks.**

A young girl was sitting in the garden
She was wearing a summer dress
covered in little pink flowers. Suddenly,
a bee, which was making a lot of noise
came and sat on her dress.

"Hello, bee, said the girl.

Hi, flower," replied the bee.

The girl looked at the bee in surprise.

The girl asked, "How can you talk You're only a bee."

"How can you talk? Youre only a flower," replied the bee Then it flew away.

## Vocabulary: using the correct word

Be careful with words that sound the same but mean different things!

**1** **Rewrite the sentences correctly.**

1  Its great to see you.  _It's great to see you._

2  Do you know who's house this is?  _____

3  I've read all her books accept this one.  _____

4  The Sahara is the biggest dessert in the world.  _____

5  We could of gone to school today.  _____

6  Did you loose your phone again?  _____

**2** **Write sentences using these words.**

1  **a** bee  _____

   **b** be  _____

2  **a** warn  _____

   **b** worn  _____

3  **a** scene  _____

   **b** seen  _____

# 9

# Power of music

## Reading: comprehension
SB p.100

**Read the blog again and choose the correct option.**

1 Why does the blogger think that music can be a very powerful art form?

   **a** Because music can be quiet.       **b** Because music can be loud.

   **c** Because music can be exciting.

2 What did Band Aid do?

   **a** They made a song that helped some people.

   **b** They made a song that helped the Arctic.

   **c** They made a song that built schools for Emmanuel Jal.

3 Why did Ludovico write music about the Arctic?

   **a** Because he wanted to make money.    **b** Because he wanted to visit the Arctic.

   **c** Because he wanted to make people care about the Arctic.

## Reading: research
SB p.100

**Find out more about these items mentioned in the blog. Give your sources, too. Remember only to use sources that you trust.**

1 *Their song made a lot of noise and also made a lot of money to help people in Africa.*

   Find out more about Band Aid. Who was involved? What did they do to help? What were the results of what they did?

   _____

   _____

   Source: _____

2 *Ludovico Einaudi wanted to make people care about the fact that the Arctic is in danger.*

   Find out more about why the Arctic is in danger. What are people doing about it? How has Ludovico Einaudi's music helped?

   _____

   _____

   Source: _____

3 *Emmanuel Jal has now helped a lot of charities.*

   Find out about what charities Emmanuel Jal has helped. In what ways has he used his music to help other people?

   _____

   _____

   Source: _____

## Vocabulary: words in context

SB p.102

Complete the text with the correct form of the words from the box.

> issue    survive    perform    charity    pay attention    environmental

Music makes people ¹ _____ to important ² _____ and

social ³ _____. For example, last month musicians ⁴ _____ a

concert to support a local ⁵ _____. They made a lot of money to help people

who ⁶ _____ last year's hurricane.

## Use of English: verbs + prepositions

SB p.102

**1** Complete the sentences with the correct form of the verbs from the box + *about* or *with*.

> disagree    care    ~~share~~    complain    dream    communicate

**1** I don't have my own computer – this is the computer I <u>share with</u> my sister.

**2** He _____ the environment – it's very important to him.

**3** My parents have different opinions from me – I _____ them.

**4** Our teacher is good at telling us information – he _____ us very well.

**5** I _____ moving to the USA – I really hope it happens one day.

**6** Sarah's soup was cold – she _____ it and the waiter brought her another bowl.

**2** Complete the sentences with the correct preposition and your own ideas.

**1** I dream _____ .

**2** I care _____ .

**3** I disagree _____ .

## Use of English: relative clauses

SB p.102

Complete the sentences with the correct relative pronoun.

1 This is the town <u>where</u> we used to live.

2 People _____ don't like children shouldn't be teachers.

3 My grandparents live in Spain. That's _____ I moved here.

4 It was summer _____ we went to the beach.

5 The car is a form of transport _____ is bad for the environment.

## Use of English: relative clauses with *whose*

SB p.102

**1** **Look at this sentence from the blog and complete the grammar rule.**

*Think about the people* **whose** *lives we can change.*

We use the word *whose* in defining relative clauses as:

**a** an object pronoun

**b** a subject pronoun

**c** a possessive pronoun

**2** **Complete the sentences with *who* or *whose*.**

**1** I met a girl _____ mother works at our school.

**2** I met a girl _____ used to go to our school.

**3** Simon and Jerome are the boys _____ visited me last week.

**4** Simon and Jerome are the boys _____ ball I found in the garden.

**5** This is the woman _____ sister is on TV.

**6** This is the woman _____ is on TV.

## Vocabulary: feelings

SB p.103

Complete the sentences with the adjectives from the box.

| relaxed | stressed | lonely | miserable | embarrassed | cheerful |

**1** I feel very _____ because I have a test tomorrow and I really want to

do well. After the test is over, I'll feel _____ because I'll have nothing to worry about!

**2** Guyaume was very unhappy last week – he was _____ because his cat was

missing. But today the cat came home and he's very _____ again.

**3** I felt very _____ on the bus today because I didn't have anyone to talk to. Then I fell over when I was getting off the bus in front of lots of people and that made me feel _____.

## Use of English: reported questions

SB p.104

Complete the table with direct and reported questions.

| Direct question | Reported question |
|---|---|
| He asked me, "Where do you come from?" | **1** <u>He asked me where I came from.</u> |
| **2** _____ | She asked if I would help her. |
| Sarah asked Dominic, "Are you learning the piano or the guitar?" | **3** _____ |
| **4** _____ | Janie asked her friend what her favourite song was. |
| Mark asked his mother, "Did you see my music homework yesterday?" | **5** _____ |
| **6** _____ | Pierre asked his cousin whether he preferred classical music or pop music. |

## Writing: punctuation

SB p.104

**1** **Read the *Punctuation tip* and add the missing punctuation into the sentences below.**

**1** What time does your music lesson start she asked her friend

**2** They asked their teacher Are we going to play in the school concert

**3** Did you practise this song Janus asked his friend

**4** What's your favourite instrument he asked Bader

> ### Punctuation tip
> Note the position of commas and question marks in the following direct questions.
>
> *"What do you want to listen to?" Otis asked his friend.*
>
> *He asked them, "Do you listen to the radio or MP3 player?"*

**2** Write these reported questions as direct questions. Remember to use the correct punctuation.

**1** He asked me what time I would be home. <u>"What time will you be home?" he asked me.</u>

**2** Kim asked her sister if she wanted a drink.

_____

**3** Leo asked Mina where his coat was.

_____

**4** Sophie asked her friend whether she was cold.

_____

## Focus on Music: instrument families in an orchestra

SB p.106

Write the instrument name and the instrument family it belongs to.

**1**

<u>tuba, brass</u>

**2**

_____ _____

**3**

_____ _____

**4**

_____ _____

**5**

_____ _____

**6**

_____ _____

**7**

_____ _____

**8**

_____ _____

---

### Check your progress

**1 What can you do now?**

I can …

read and talk about the power of music ☐

use defining relative clauses ☐

use reported questions ☐

understand speakers' opinions ☐

talk and write about whether music is important ☐

**2 Answer the questions about this unit.**

**1** What have you enjoyed most?

_____

**2** Is there anything you have found difficult?

_____

**3** What would you like to learn more about?

_____

### My learning

What did you learn in this unit?

# 10

**City life**

## Vocabulary: useful adjectives

SB p.110

Complete the sentences with the adjectives from the box.

| local | knowledgeable | lively |
| experienced | peaceful | convenient |

1 My cousin knows a lot about the history and culture of the city – he is

very _____ about it.

2 We stayed in a quiet hotel in the country – it was very _____.

3 The hotel is very _____ because it's near the centre of town and the train station.

4 We don't want to go far from the hotel – do you know any good _____ restaurants?

5 This area is very _____ – there are two theatres, a cinema and a lot of restaurants and cafes.

6 The tour guide has been doing his job for 20 years – he's very _____.

## Use of English: reported commands

SB p.111

**1** Complete the reported commands.

1 Marta to me: "Get off the bed!"

Marta told me _____ .

2 Sam to Rachel: "Don't close the door!"

Sam told Rachel _____ .

3 The teacher to us: "Write down the words!"

The teacher told _____ .

4 Peter to his baby brother: "Don't eat the sock!"

Peter told _____ .

5 Valerie to James: "Give me the book!"

Valerie _____ .

6 Laura to Nina: "Don't tell me the answer!"

Laura _____ .

**2** Rewrite the sentences in bold as reported commands.

Tara:     [1] **Look at this article!** There's a new exhibition at the museum.

Laura:    Oh yes, it looks good. Shall we go on Saturday?

Tara:     No, I can't. I'm going away on Friday.

**Laura:** Oh yes. <sup>2</sup> **Don't forget to send me a postcard!** We could go when you get back.

**Tara:** <sup>3</sup> **Don't worry about me.** I don't really want to go anyway. <sup>4</sup> **Go with Sarah.**

**Laura:** OK, I'll give her a ring.<sup>5</sup> **Pass me the phone.**

1 *Tara told Laura to look at that article.* _____

2 _____

3 _____

4 _____

5 _____

## Vocabulary: a great city

SB p.112

**1** Write the phrases in the box next to the correct definitions or examples.

> lively, exciting culture    beautiful, original architecture    parks and open spaces
> interesting, friendly people    reliable transport system    plenty of job opportunities

1 Good roads, buses, trains and taxis: _____

2 Good theatres, cafes, restaurants, museums and art galleries: _____

3 Green areas with trees and grass: _____

4 Good employment for people: _____

5 Well designed buildings: _____

6 Nice men and women who make you feel welcome: _____

**2** Answer the questions. Use vocabulary from Activity 1.
1 Which of these things do you think is most important in a city? Why?

_____

2 Which of these things do you think is least important in a city? Why?

_____

## Reading: comprehension SB p.113

Read the three tweets about the article. Which do you think describes it best?

1

**Tweet** @tweet  👤 Follow

Interesting survey about why people who live in cities are happier than people in the country.

2
**Tweet** @tweet  👤 Follow

Great read about the five most important cities in the world.

3

**Tweet** @tweet  👤 Follow

Check out this article about what people look for in great cities.

## Reading: thinking about the text SB p.113

Think about the survey results by answering questions about the place where you live.

1 Does the place where you live have a lively culture? Why? Why not?

_____

2 What sort of job opportunities are there?

_____

3 What's your favourite open space and why?

_____

4 Is there a reliable transport system? Why? Why not?

_____

5 Are there interesting, friendly people?

_____

## Vocabulary: spelling SB p.113

Find and correct six spelling mistakes.

I read a report that said that it's important to get away from the stres of city life sometimes and that this can have great health benifits. So, last week, I took some time out of my busy day to go to an exibition at a local art galery. As I was looking at a picture, I realised that a stranjer was waving at me from the other side of the room. He was some distanse away from me and I didn't recognise him. As he came closer, I realised that it was my old art teacher from school! We were happy to see each other again and looked at the pictures together!

1 _____  2 _____  3 _____

4 _____  5 _____  6 _____

## Use of English: infinitive after adjectives and verbs SB p.114

**1** Match the words with a similar meaning.

| | | | |
|---|---|---|---|
| **1** shocked | | **a** seem | |
| **2** likely | | **b** surprised | |
| **3** certain | | **c** sure | |
| **4** appear | | **d** probable | |
| **5** continue | | **e** wait to happen | |
| **6** expect | | **f** not stop | |

**2** Put the words in the correct order to make sentences.

**1** shocked / brother. / was / to / The / see / girl / her

_____

**2** to / at / We / arrive / three o'clock. / expect

_____

**3** appears / open. / The / art gallery / to / be

_____

**4** by / The / train. / students / travel / continued / to

_____

**5** until / Are / Friday? / you / to / likely / stay

_____

**6** arrive / post / tomorrow. / The / in / letter / certain / is / to / the

_____

## Use of English: noun phrases SB p.114

Complete the sentences with the noun phrases.

| | | |
|---|---|---|
| sitting in the corner | that I bought yesterday | with peanut butter |
| my six favourite | with the blue door | |

**1** Do you like the dress _____?

**2** These are _____ films.

**3** Did you see the boy _____?

**4** I work in the office _____.

**5** I love eating sandwiches _____.

**1** **Match the cities to the countries.**

1 Munich
2 Vienna
3 Auckland
4 Vancouver
5 Zurich

a Austria
b New Zealand
c Switzerland
d Germany
e Canada

**2** **Complete the missing letters to make words relating to the quality of life in a city.**

☐ p_lit_cs
☐ ec_no_ics
☐ soc_al free_om
☐ heal_h ce_tres
☐ ed_cati_n

☐ tra_spo_t
☐ c_ltu_e
☐ sh_ps
☐ h_use_
☐ nat_ral en_iron_ent

**3** **What do you think is important for quality of life in a city? Rank the words in Activity 2 from 1 (most important) to 10 (least important).**

*Check your progress*

1 **What can you do now?**

I can …

talk and write about city and country life ☐

use reported commands ☐

understand the detail of speakers' and writers' arguments ☐

give a presentation about my favourite city ☐

write a description of my favourite city ☐

**My learning**
What did you learn in this unit?

2 **Answer the questions about this unit.**

1 What have you enjoyed most?

_____

2 Is there anything you have found difficult?

_____

3 What would you like to learn more about?

_____

# A job for life

## Reading: comprehension
**SB p.122**

Read the text again and write *True, False* or *Doesn't Say*. Correct any sentences that are false.

**1** Nurses are happier than doctors in their jobs. _____

**2** People who earn a lot of money are happier than those who don't. _____

**3** Farmers are happier than lawyers. _____

**4** The teacher thinks that children are amusing and clever. _____

**5** The nurse doesn't mind working long hours. _____

**6** The doctor doesn't work with other people very often. _____

## Reading: research
**SB p.122**

**Find out more about one of the jobs mentioned in the article. Give your sources. Remember only to use sources that you trust. Find out:**

• how you learn to do this job

• what a typical day is like.

_____

_____

_____

_____

Sources: _____

## Vocabulary: multi-word verbs with *put*
**SB p.123**

**Complete the multi-word verbs with *put*.**

**1** Could you put the washing machine _____, please.

**2** The firefighter put the fire _____ quickly.

**3** Could you put me _____ to Mr Harris, please?

**4** I've put all the boxes _____ in the cupboard for you.

**5** My teacher put the exam _____ until next week because we missed two whole lessons.

**6** I put my suitcase _____ while I was standing in the queue.

## Vocabulary: jobs

**1** Match the jobs with the pictures.

| designer    lawyer    scientist    vet    musician    firefighter |

1 _____  2 _____  3 _____

4 _____  5 _____  6 _____

**2** Write a sentence to describe what these people do.

**1** A designer _____

**2** A lawyer _____

**3** A scientist _____

**4** A vet _____

**5** A musician _____

**6** A firefighter _____

**3** Copy and complete the sentences about the jobs from Activity 1.

**1** I think the most interesting job is a _____ because _____.

**2** I think the most important job is a _____ because _____.

**3** I would most like to become a _____ because _____.

## Vocabulary: talking about jobs

SB p.125

**1** **Replace the underlined words in the text with the words from the box.**

| part-time job | salary | training | career | work experience |

I'm still not sure what I want do to as my job in life [1] _____ . Last week, I did some work for a company for a short period of time to see if I liked it [2] _____ at a hospital. I will have to do many years of learning about how to do the job [3] _____ if I want to be a doctor. I might get a job where I work for part of each week [4] _____ and the money that I earn from the job [5] _____ can go towards my studies.

**2** **Answer the questions.**

1 What *training* do you need to do to follow the *career* you want?

_____

2 Where would you like to do *work experience* and why?

_____

3 If you could have any *part-time job* in the world, what would you choose and why?

_____

4 Is a good *salary* important to you in a job?

_____

## Use of English: asking questions politely

SB p.126

**Rewrite the questions to make them more polite.**

1 What time does the shop close?

Do you know _____

2 When can you start work experience?

Could _____

3 What's the company name?

I wonder _____

4 Is the station this way?

Could _____

5 Is there a bank near here?

I wonder _____

## Use of English: using modal verbs

**1** **Read and choose the correct option below.**

**Lynn:** Dad, I've got my first day of work experience tomorrow – ¹ _____ you give me some tips?

**Dad:** Of course. You ² _____ wear jeans, that's for sure. It ³ _____ be OK to wear casual clothes for some jobs, but you ⁴ _____ always try to look smart for work experience.

**Lynn:** Dad, ⁵ _____ you drive me tomorrow? I ⁶ _____ be late if I take the train.

**Dad:** Yes, of course

**Lynn:** Thanks Dad.

1 **a** should          **b** may not          **c** could          **d** might not

2 **a** might          **b** would          **c** may not          **d** shouldn't

3 **a** may not          **b** might          **c** shouldn't          **d** would

4 **a** should          **b** may          **c** might not          **d** could

5 **a** shouldn't          **b** would          **c** may not          **d** wouldn't

6 **a** should          **b** might          **c** may not          **d** wouldn't

**2** **Use a modal verb to complete the second sentence so that it means the same as the first.**

1 It's possible that I will get a job over the summer.

I _____ get a job over the summer.

2 It would be a good idea if I wear smart clothes.

I _____ wear smart clothes.

3 It would be a bad idea for you to give up the piano.

You _____ give up the piano.

# Focus on Maths: analysing data

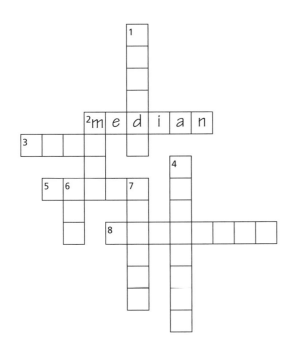

## Across

**2** the number that is in the middle of a set of numbers

**3** the number that appears most often in a set

**5** the difference between the lowest and highest number in a set

**8** the word for ×

## Down

**1** the word for ÷

**2** the result of adding a set of numbers together and dividing them by the number of things

**4** the word for −

**6** the word for +

**7** the word for =

---

*Check your progress*

**1 What can you do now?**

I can …

listen to and take part in a job interview ☐

use modal verbs ☐

use polite questions ☐

talk about and write a description of my dream job ☐

work out the mean, median, mode and range in maths ☐

carry out a survey and analyse the data ☐

**2 Answer the questions about this unit.**

**1** What have you enjoyed most?

_____

**2** Is there anything you have found difficult?

_____

**3** What would you like to learn more about?

_____

### My learning

What did you learn in this unit?

# 12 Helping hand

## Vocabulary: words in context

SB p.132

**1** Complete the text with the words in the box.

| charity | kindness | duty | care | stranger | involved |

I think it's our ¹ _____ to our community to give something back and

show the people around us that we ² _____ . So, I decided to get

³ _____ in a local ⁴ _____ . For the last three months, I've been

helping out at the local food bank, which hands out food parcels to people who need

them. Showing a bit of ⁵ _____ to a ⁶ _____ always makes my day.

**2** Answer the questions.

**1** Do you think it's our duty to show people we care? Why? Why not?

_____

**2** Are you involved in any local charities? Would you like to be? Give details.

_____

**3** How do you feel when you show kindness to a stranger?

_____

## Use of English: using modal verbs

SB p.133

**1** Complete the sentences with *must, have to, mustn't* or *don't have to*.

**1** We have a school uniform – we _____ wear our own clothes to school.

**2** I strongly suggest you listen – you _____ pay attention.

**3** We aren't allowed to leave our bikes here – we _____ move them.

**4** You can decide what you want to do – you _____ come with us.

**5** You need to stay in bed until you're better – you _____ get up.

**6** We're late – we _____ leave now.

**2** Choose the correct options.

**1** I strongly believe in helping people. We [must / don't have to] show others that we care.

**2** You aren't allowed coffee in the classroom. You [must / mustn't] drink it in here.

**3** It's up to you whether you order a suspended coffee. You [have to / don't have to] buy one.

**4** We need to clear away our cups. We [have to / don't have to] leave the kitchen tidy.

**Read the text again and match questions and answers.**

1 How does the environmental charity protect forests?

2 What types of animals does the animal charity rescue?

3 What does the animal charity do to people who are unkind to animals?

4 How do art workshops help people who can't talk?

5 What does the arts charity help people to do through drama?

6 What does sport do in divided communities?

a It reports them to the police.

b It helps them to find a voice.

c It stops people cutting them down and plants new trees.

d It helps them to find hope after difficult experiences.

e It brings people together.

f Animals that are in danger.

## Reading: research | SB p.134

**Write about a charity that you would like to support. Find out what it does and what its main aims are. Complete the box and remember to use the correct punctuation for bullet points.**

Name: _____

This charity _____

- _____

- _____

- _____

## Punctuation: bullet points | SB p.135

**Rewrite this sentence as a bullet-point list.**

*Lists are useful because we can write lots of different ideas, they make us check we aren't saying the same thing twice and they are easy to read.*

## Vocabulary: words in context

SB p.135

Complete the crossword with the missing words from the sentences. What is the vertical word in the grey boxes and what does it mean?

|   |   |
|---|---|
| 1 | |
| 2 | |
| 3 | |
| 4 | |
| 5 | |

**Hidden word:**

Meaning: _____

_____

_____

1 Everyone should be able to use libraries – we should all have a _____ to them.

2 We tried to p_____ the injured bird and keep it safe until we got to the vet.

3 The firefighter tried to r_____ the cat, which was stuck up a tree.

4 The city is d_____ and the two parts are quite different.

5 They are building a new classroom for d_____ children, which will have facilities that are specially designed for their needs.

## Use of English: pronouns *somebody, nothing, anyone,* etc...

SB p.135

**1** Complete the table with the missing pronouns.

|         | –one            | –body           | –thing          |
|---------|-----------------|-----------------|-----------------|
| every–  | 1 _____   | 2 _____   | everything      |
| some–   | 3 _____   | somebody        | 4 _____   |
| any–    | anyone          | 5 _____   | 6 _____   |
| no–     | 7 _____   | 8 _____   | nothing         |

**2** Complete the sentences with one of the pronouns from Activity 1.

1 I really want to do _____ to help out at my local food bank.

2 Is there _____ here who can volunteer on Saturday?

3 _____ cares about these animals any more so they are dying out.

4 We are all doing _____ we possibly can to help.

5 Sam wanted to help his friend move house, but there was _____ for him to do, so he went home.

6 _____ in the school took part in the race for charity and they raised a lot of money.

# Use of English: likely and unlikely conditionals

SB p.136

**1** Complete the likely conditional sentences with the correct form of the verb in brackets.

1 If I _____ (go) to the gym this afternoon, I'll sleep better tonight.

2 If I find your keys, I _____ (give) you a ring to let you know.

3 If I have time, I _____ (volunteer) at a charity shop.

4 It will be better for the environment if we _____ (travel) by train.

5 If we _____ (not / hurry), we'll miss the start of the film.

6 I _____ (tell) John your news if I see him.

**2** Use the prompts to write unlikely conditional sentences.

1 if / I / win the lottery / give some money to charity

_____

2 if / Tom / speak French / get a job in Paris

_____

3 we / buy a new car / if / be rich

_____

4 Sam / feel better / if / eat a healthy diet

_____

5 if / I / find a phone in the street / take it to the police station

_____

6 If / Emma and Ian / not have a fish / get a cat

_____

**3** Choose the correct option to complete the conditional sentences.

1 If I (see / saw) Mario today, I (will / would) give him the message.

2 If I (have / had) a million pounds, I (will / would) give it to an animal charity.

3 Ben (will / would) go to university next year if he (passes / passed) his exams.

4 If it (doesn't cost / didn't cost) so much money, we (will / would) visit New York.

5 If Xi (isn't / wasn't) so busy, she (will / would) help at the charity event.

6 If I (have / had) enough money tomorrow, I (will / would) buy a suspended coffee at lunchtime.

**1** **Complete the sentences with the words in the box.**

> friendship     strength     courage     character     greatness

**1** Isla felt afraid, but she found the _____ to tell the police what had happened.

**2** My grandma's _____ with her best friend has lasted for 45 years, since they first met.

**3** Ben is hoping to achieve _____ with his new business ideas.

**4** My father has got a lot of _____, and he was able to pick up the extremely heavy chair.

**5** Grant's _____ seems to have changed – he used to be very shy but now he speaks to everyone.

**2** **Answer the questions.**

**1** What did you enjoy about reading the extracts from *Wonder*?

_____

**2** What did you learn from reading the extracts from *Wonder*?

_____

**3** Would you like to read the rest of the book? Why? Why not?

_____

**3** **Complete the sentences.**

This week, I'm going to be kind at school by _____

I'm going to be kind at home by _____

---

***Check your progress***

**1 What can you do now?**

I can …

listen to a podcast about being kind to other people    ☐

use modal verbs    ☐

use likely and unlikely conditionals    ☐

read about different charities and talk about which one to support    ☐

write a letter to my head teacher about my chosen charity    ☐

do a kindness project to make the world a better place    ☐

**2 Answer the questions about this unit.**

**1** What have you enjoyed most? _____

**2** Is there anything you have found difficult? _____

**3** What would you like to learn more about? _____

***My learning***

What did you learn in this unit?

## Reading: understanding specific information

**SB p.145**

**Read the blog again and match.**

1 When she checked Facebook,

2 When she checked Twitter,

3 When she checked Instagram,

4 She admits that

5 She tried to give up her phone, but

a she was disappointed that nobody had replied to her tweet.

b she is a smartphone addict.

c she was upset that nobody had commented on her video of a cat.

d she wasn't very successful.

e she was unhappy about a party that she hadn't been invited to.

## Reading: thinking about the text

**SB p.145**

**Answer the questions.**

1 Do you think it's a good idea to check social media before you get up in the morning? Why? Why not?

_____

2 Are you nomophobic? Do you know anyone who is nomophobic? Are you addicted to any other form of technology?

_____

3 Were you surprised by the results of the report mentioned in the text? Why? Why not?

_____

4 Have you ever tried to give up some form of technology? What happened? Would you like to try?

_____

## Punctuation: possessives

**SB p.145**

**Add the missing apostrophes.**

1 I have two brothers who share a computer. This is my brothers computer.
  *I have two brothers who share a computer. This is my brothers' computer.*

2 I have one brother who has his own computer. This is my brothers computer.

3 This phone belongs to the girl. This is the girls phone.

4 This office belongs to our head teacher. The head teachers office is large.

5 All the students did very well in the exam. The students exam results were very good.

**1** Choose the correct option to complete the sentences.

1 When you _____ something, you take some form of information that someone else has posted and you make it visible to all of your friends or the people who follow you.

  **a** share           **b** comment           **c** update

2 When you _____ information or a photo, you put it online so that other people can see it.

  **a** comment        **b** post *or* upload       **c** update

3 When you _____ on something on a social media site, you add to the conversation.

  **a** post            **b** comment          **c** share

4 On Twitter you can _____ your own message and you can _____ other people's messages.

  **a** share / comment on    **b** tweet / retweet      **c** like / update

5 When you _____ something on social media, you are saying that you think something is good.

  **a** like             **b** comment          **c** upload

6 When you _____ a website or status, you add the latest information.

  **a** like             **b** comment          **c** update

**2** All the verb options in Activity 1 can also be used as nouns. Look at the example below using *share*. Choose four more verbs from Activity 1 and write sentences using them as nouns.

Example: <u>My photo of a funny fish got 123 shares!</u>

1 _____

2 _____

3 _____

4 _____

**3** Read and match.

1 Facebook      **a** is a social media site where users share photographs, which are deleted as soon as they are viewed.

2 Twitter        **b** is mainly a video-sharing social media site.

3 Instagram     **c** is a social media site where users create profiles, upload photos and videos, send messages and keep in touch with friends.

4 Snapchat     **d** is mainly a photo-sharing social media site.

5 YouTube      **e** is a social media site where users post short messages of 140 characters or less.

# Use of English: talking about regrets

**1** **Read the first sentence. Then, complete the second sentence to show regret.**

**1** I haven't got my phone, so I can't call my mum.

I wish _____ my phone.

**2** Mario didn't take any photographs and now he feels sad about it.

He should _____ some photographs.

**3** The students forgot their passwords and couldn't do their work.

The students shouldn't _____ their passwords.

**4** I didn't help my sister and now I feel bad.

I should _____ my sister.

**5** I went to bed very late last night, so I'm really tired.

I wish _____ so late last night.

**6** You missed the presentation, so you can't do the homework.

You shouldn't _____ the presentation.

**2** **Complete the sentences with your own ideas.**

**1** I'm tired – I wish _____

**2** I didn't study for this exam – I should _____

**3** You're late for school – you shouldn't _____

**4** The shop is closed now – if only it _____

**3** **Write three things that you regret doing or not doing.**

**1** _____

**2** _____

**3** _____

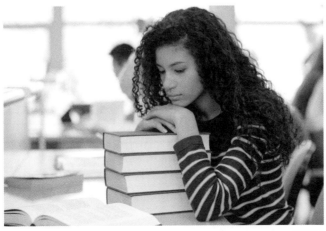

## Vocabulary: abstract nouns

**Find six abstract nouns in the wordsearch. Write them next to the definitions below.**

| s | r | t | t | u | s | m | o | k | x | v |
|---|---|---|---|---|---|---|---|---|---|---|
| h | a | p | p | i | n | e | s | s | s | i |
| n | a | z | t | r | e | c | u | f | a | d |
| v | v | e | t | z | l | o | c | r | b | l |
| o | p | p | o | r | t | u | n | i | t | y |
| s | z | a | r | t | y | h | v | a | v | e |
| x | o | n | x | t | h | o | u | g | h | t |
| s | d | p | d | a | n | g | e | r | g | s |
| h | w | i | s | a | d | n | e | s | s | s |
| e | y | n | b | s | u | c | c | e | s | s |
| s | z | o | y | r | o | v | c | u | o | q |

1 <u>thought</u>: an idea or opinion

2 _____: when you do well and get the result you wanted

3 _____: something that can hurt or harm you

4 _____: a situation in which it is possible for you to do something you want to do

5 _____: a feeling of pleasure or satisfaction

6 _____: a feeling of unhappiness

## Vocabulary: multi-word verbs

SB p.148

**Complete the sentences with the correct form of *give* + a preposition from the box below.**

> in (×2)    away    out    up    ~~back~~

1 Denita <u>gave back</u> my scarf, which she had borrowed.

2 The students _____ their essays tomorrow.

3 They _____ free coffees in the shopping centre today, so we didn't have to pay!

4 Rita _____ and agreed to go to the concert last weekend even though she didn't really want to.

5 I _____ chocolate for three months last year – I really missed it!

6 Will you please _____ the books to all the students, Hannah?

## Focus on ICT

SB pp.150–151

**1 Complete the sentences with the words in the box.**

> click    personal    junk    password    phishing
> identity    privacy    cyberbullying    spam    virus

1 Don't tell anyone your _____ or they will be able to access your emails.

2 I was a victim of _____ theft last week – someone used my name to buy something online.

**3** Don't enter your _____ information unless the website is secure.

**4** If you _____ on this link, it will take you to the website you're looking for.

**5** Make sure that your _____ settings are set up, so that strangers can't look at your account.

**6** I'm sick of getting so many _____ emails trying to sell me things I don't want.

**7** My sister is a victim of _____ – people are posting horrible messages about her online.

**8** I think my computer has a _____ because it's not working properly.

**9** I received a _____ email yesterday trying to get me to reveal my personal information.

**10** My _____ folder is full of spam and phishing emails.

**2** **Write three things you can do to help you to stay safe online.**

**1** _____

**2** _____

**3** _____

### Check your progress

**1 What can you do now?**

I can …

understand a blog about mobile phone addiction ☐

talk about regrets ☐

use multi-word verbs ☐

talk and write about the advantages and disadvantages of growing up in the digital age ☐

stay safe online ☐

**2 Answer the questions about this unit.**

**1** What have you enjoyed most?

_____

**2** Is there anything you have found difficult?

_____

**3** What would you like to learn more about?

_____

### My learning

What did you learn in this unit?

## Reading: comprehension
SB pp.154–155

Read the signs again and correct the mistakes in these sentences. One sentence doesn't have any mistakes.

**Sign 1:** There's a special offer today for $2.99.

_____

**Sign 2:** There are bigger reductions on beds than there are on sofas.

_____

**Sign 3:** This sale is on clothes from the new season.

_____

**Sign 4:** This sale is happening on a Tuesday.

_____

**Sign 5:** You can buy one suitcase, but pay for two.

_____

## Writing: shop signs
SB pp.154–155

Read the situations and write shop signs. Use expressions from the shop signs in the Student's Book.

**1** Electronics shop: 10% off mobile phones

**2** Bed shop: closing-down sale

## Vocabulary: sales
SB pp.154–155

Find words on the signs that have the following meanings.

**1** a price that is lower than it usually is: _special offer_

**2** a reduction in the usual price of something: _____

**3** another word for a shop: _____

**4** an adjective that means small in size or number: _____

**5** a word that means an arrangement of things in a shop: _____

**6** when something is made smaller or less than it was before: _____

**7** when a shop stops working as a business: _____

**8** a word that means the total amount of goods that a shop has available to sell: _____

# Use of English: talking about quantity

SB p.156

**1** **Look and write.**

1

two loaves of b_____

2

one item of c_____

3

one carton of j_____

4

two slices of c_____

5

three bars of c_____

6

one piece of f_____

**2** **Choose the correct options.**

**1** Could I have two _____ of tea, please?
  **a** cups      **b** bars      **c** loaves

**2** There's a _____ of milk in the fridge.
  **a** slice      **b** piece      **c** bottle

**3** I'd like four _____ of bread, please.
  **a** bottles      **b** slices      **c** bars

**4** Do we need a _____ of orange juice?
  **a** bar      **b** piece      **c** carton

**5** Could you pass me a _____ of paper, please?
  **a** piece      **b** slice      **c** bar

**6** Would you like a _____ of chocolate?
  **a** loaf      **b** bottle      **c** bar

**3** **Write three sentences using words from the box. Use your imagination.**

| slice | piece | item | bar | loaf | carton |
|-------|-------|------|-----|------|--------|

1 _____

2 _____

3 _____

## Writing: spelling

SB p.156

Look at the Spelling tip in your Student's Book on page 156, then correct the spelling mistakes below. One sentence is already correct.

1 I have lost two scarfs this year. _____

2 The thiefs escaped out of the window. _____

3 I've put up some new shelfs. _____

4 The roofs on these houses are old. _____

5 I cleared up the leaves from the path. _____

6 I saw two wolfs in the forest. _____

## Vocabulary: useful expressions for sales

SB p.156

Choose the correct prepositions to complete the signs.

Come and see what we have ¹[in / on] sale! 15% ²[under / off] all shoes!!
Many items of clothing ³[in / at] half price!

*Hundreds of special offers ⁴[in / into] store today!!*
*Cartons of milk: two ⁵[at / for] the price ⁶[of / on] one*

New furniture ⁷[on / in] stock now! Sofas ⁸[down by / down in] 10%!
Come and see what we have ⁹[in / on] display!

## Vocabulary: advertising

SB p.157

Match words and definitions.

1 taste (n)          a something you make or grow in order to sell it
2 influence (n)      b affect what someone does or what happens.
3 product (n)        c give all your attention to
4 focus on (v)       d grow or change over a period of time
5 encourage (v)      e give someone hope or confidence
6 develop (v)        f someone's choice in all the things they like or buy

## Use of English: *so that, in order to, to*

SB p.158

Review the example sentences in the table. Then use the words in brackets to join the sentences in 1 to 6 below..

| | Positive sentences | |
|---|---|---|
| I went online | **in order to** do some research for science. | |
| | **to** do some shopping. | |
| | **so that** I could chat with my friends. | |
| | Negative sentences | |
| I ran fast | **in order not to** miss the bus. | |
| | **so as not to** be late for school. | |
| | **so that** I didn't come last in the race. | |

1 I moved to Spain. I wanted to learn Spanish.  (*in order to*)
   I moved to Spain in order to learn Spanish.

2 I joined a new social media website. I wanted to chat to friends. (*to*)

3 Lisa exercises every day. She wants to stay healthy. (*so that*)

4 The boys are studying very hard. They don't want to fail their exams. (*in order not to*)

5 I put on a jumper. I didn't want to be cold. (*so as not to*)

6 I put the appointment in my phone. I didn't want to forget about it. (*so that*)


## Use of English: compound adjectives

SB p.158

Complete the sentences with compound adjectives from the box.

| | | | |
|---|---|---|---|
| fast-changing | thousand-dollar | 15-year-old | ~~middle-aged~~ |
| | up-to-date | 30-second | |

1 My parents are in their forties. They are middle-aged people.

2 This website changes very fast. It's a _____ website.

3 This car cost thousands of dollars. It's a _____ car.

4 This advert lasts 30 seconds. It's a _____ advert.

5 I've got the new phone that has just been released. It's an _____ phone.

6 My brother is 15. He's a _____ boy.

## Focus on the World

SB pp.160–161

**Read the article again and answer the questions.**

1 Why did people get excited about the photograph of the bird in South Africa?

_____

2 What did the video that was posted by BirdLife South Africa reveal?

_____

3 What sort of art do the artists of Washed Ashore make?

_____

4 What do they use to make this art?

_____

5 What did David Walliams do to raise awareness and money for charity?

_____

6 What did the flash mob in China teach people?

_____

---

**Check your progress**

1 **What can you do now?**

I can …

understand shop signs ☐

use *so that, in order to* and *to* ☐

use compound adjectives ☐

talk about adverts and advertising ☐

write a product review ☐

make my own advertisement ☐

**My learning**
What did you learn in this unit?

2 **Answer the questions about this unit.**

1 What have you enjoyed most?

_____

2 Is there anything you have found difficult?

_____

3 What would you like to learn more about?

_____

**Reading: comprehension**

SB pp.166–167

**1** Read the article again and complete the table.

|  | Raymond Wang | Lalita Prasida Sripada Srisai | Anurudh Ganesan |
|---|---|---|---|
| Where are they from? | 1 _____ | 5 _____ | 9 _____ |
| What did they invent? | 2 _____ _____ _____ | 6 _____ _____ | 10 _____ _____ _____ |
| How old were they at the time? | 3 _____ | 7 _____ | 11 _____ |
| Why is their invention important? | 4 _____ _____ _____ | 8 _____ _____ _____ | 12 _____ _____ _____ |

**2** Explain how each person's invention works.

**1** Raymond Wang:

_____

**2** Lalita Prasida Sripada Srisai:

_____

**3** Anurudh Ganesan:

_____

**Reading: research**

SB pp.166–167

Research another teenage inventor. Find answers to the questions in the table in Activity 1 above and write a paragraph to add to the article.

_____

_____

_____

_____

_____

## Vocabulary: useful verbs and nouns

SB p.168

Complete the sentences with the words from the box.

| vaccines | filters | spreading | attaching | germs |
|----------|---------|-----------|-----------|-------|

**1** Raymond's invention stops _____ from _____ .

**2** Lalita hopes that her invention, which _____ water, will be used in places where people don't have clean water.

**3** Anurudh's invention is a way of _____ a bicycle to a plastic cooler, which means that _____ can be kept cool.

## Use of English: relative clauses with prepositions

SB p.168

Read and match.

**1** Raymond is the inventor          **a** in which he made his invention.

**2** That's the building               **b** whom she is speaking invented this watch.

**3** The man with                      **c** to whom we gave the award.

**4** The bicycle                       **d** for which the inventor received no prizes, has changed the world.

**5** The aeroplanes in                 **e** on which you are sitting could be used to transport medicines.

**6** This invention,                   **f** which we travel can cause the spread of diseases.

## Use of English: verb + –ing form or verb + to + verb

SB p.168

**1** Write the words from the box under the correct heading in the table below.

| imagine | consider | appear | continue | manage | prefer |
|---------|----------|--------|----------|--------|--------|

| intend | avoid | offer |

| followed by –ing form | followed by to + verb | followed by –ing form or to + verb |
|---|---|---|
| 1 _____ | 4 _____ | 7 _____ |
| 2 _____ | 5 _____ | 8 _____ |
| 3 _____ | 6 _____ | 9 _____ |

**2** Check that you know how to use the verbs in Activity 1. Write a sentence to use each of the nine verbs.

1 _____

2 _____

3 _____

4 _____

5 _____

6 _____

7 _____

8 _____

9 _____

**3** Complete the sentences with the correct form of the verb.

1 Will you consider _____ (stay) another day?

2 I didn't manage _____ (finish) my homework.

3 Do you prefer _____ (do) winter sports or summer sports?

4 He continued _____ (learn) the piano.

5 I always avoid _____ (eat) seafood.

6 He offered _____ (drive) me home.

## Vocabulary: inventions

Complete the text with the words from the box.

> discovery    potential    transform
>
> significant    technology    ~~development~~

What do I think was the most important [1] _development_ in medicine in the twentieth century? [2] _____ has been very important with the invention of laser surgery and 3-D printing. But I would have to say that the most [3] _____ thing was the [4] _____ of antibiotics by Alexander Fleming in the 1920s. Doctors quickly realised the [5] _____ of this to [6] _____ medicine and save millions of lives.

## Use of English: present perfect continuous

SB p.170

**1** Complete the sentences with the present perfect continuous form of the verb in brackets.

**1** Simon _____ (work) as a doctor for 18 years.

**2** Rita and Lauren _____ (learn) French since last September.

**3** We _____ (waiting) since 10 a.m.

**4** How long _____ (you / live) in Newcastle?

**5** Mark and I _____ (write) to each other for three years.

**6** Louis _____ (clean) his car for two hours.

**2** Correct the mistakes in these sentences. One sentence is correct.

**1** Jon have been travelling around India for four weeks.

**2** How long have you being playing the guitar?

**3** We've been standing in the rain for two hours.

**4** Emma has been looked for new shoes all afternoon.

**5** We has been working very hard on our Maths this term.

**6** Where has you been staying this week?

**3** Write questions. Then answer for you.

**1** How long / you / learn English?

_____     _____

**2** How long / you / live in your home?

_____     _____

**3** How long / you / go to your school?

_____     _____

**4** How long / you / do your favourite hobby?

_____     _____

## Focus on Science

SB pp.172–173

**Read and circle the correct option.**

**1** What type of microbe causes the flu?

 **a** virus

 **b** bacteria

 **c** antibody

**2** Which of these is *not* a way of spreading infectious diseases?

    **a** drinking infected water

    **b** breathing infected air

    **c** having a vaccine

**3** Which type of cell can kill or help to kill harmful microbes?

    **a** white blood cells

    **b** red blood cells

    **c** antibodies

**4** What substances stick to microbes to make them easier to kill?

    **a** white blood cells

    **b** red blood cells

    **c** antibodies

**5** When was a modern form of immunisation first used?

    **a** 1928

    **b** many centuries ago

    **c** 1796

---

### Check your progress

**1 What can you do now?**

I can …

    read an article about teenage inventors  ☐

    use prepositions in relative clauses  ☐

    use the present perfect continuous  ☐

    write a story about an invention  ☐

    understand infectious diseases  ☐

    make and play a game about inventions  ☐

**2 Answer the questions about this unit.**

  **1** What have you enjoyed most?

    _____

  **2** Is there anything you have found difficult?

    _____

  **3** What would you like to learn more about?

    _____

### My learning

What did you learn in this unit?

## Vocabulary: useful adjectives
SB p.177

Replace the underlined sections of the text with adjectives from the box.

~~efficient~~    creative    cost-effective    impossible    reliable    exact

My robot is called Bob. It is helpful and <u>always does tasks very successfully without wasting time or energy</u> [1] _efficient_. In the morning, it makes my breakfast. I like exactly 200 ml of milk on my cereal. It never gets this wrong because it is <u>accurate</u> [2] _____ in everything it does. It does all my shopping for me, which is always <u>good because he gets a lot of things for the money</u> [3] _____. It is also <u>a good machine that never breaks down</u> [4] _____. The only thing that it can't do is draw! It isn't very <u>good at having new ideas</u> [5] _____, but it is very useful! I think it would be <u>not possible</u> [6] _____ to find another robot, which is as good as Bob!

## Use of English: nouns + prepositions
SB p.177

Complete the sentences with the correct preposition. Then answer the questions.

1 Do you have any interest <u>in</u> having a robot that can do jobs at home?

_____

2 Have you ever read a story _____ a robot?

_____

3 What are the advantages _____ hiring a robot instead of a human to do a job?

_____

4 What are the disadvantages _____ hiring a robot instead of a human to do a job?

_____

5 What would be your reaction _____ having a robot teach you English?

_____

## Reading: comprehension SB pp.178–179

**Read and write *True*, *False* or *Doesn't say*.**

**1** Tim says that robots do a lot of work in his car factory. _____

**2** Tim says that robots can drive his cars too. _____

**3** Paula thinks that by the 2030s more than half of all jobs will be done by robots. _____

**4** Mina thinks that robots will explore space in future. _____

**5** Mina thinks that robots won't be expensive. _____

**6** Evan thinks that we should be careful when it comes to making robots intelligent. _____

## Reading: thinking about the text SB pp.178–179

**Do you agree or disagree with these statements from the article? Explain your answers.**

**1** *In the future, I think that robots are going to be used to do more and more jobs.*

_____

_____

**2** *I'm worried because robots are doing more and more of our jobs, so we are cutting down the number of jobs that are available for people to do.*

_____

_____

**3** *Robots will do all the boring jobs that humans don't want to do. This is an exciting opportunity because we can spend our time doing more interesting jobs.*

_____

_____

**4** *I believe that robots are going to be sent into space to explore.*

_____

_____

_____

**5** *There will come a point when robots will have more intelligence than humans. When that happens, there's a real risk that we will be controlled by robots.*

_____

_____

_____

## Vocabulary: abstract nouns

SB p.179

Complete the sentences with the words in the box.

> unemployment    role    opportunity
> risk    employment    intelligence

1 Robots play an important _____ in this factory.

2 Louis is a student of great _____ – I'm sure he'll pass all his exams.

3 I don't think robots will be able to do this job well, so I think it's a big _____ to use them instead of humans.

4 There are high levels of _____ in this area because there just aren't enough jobs for everyone.

5 You don't want to miss this _____ to go to Australia.

6 Mark couldn't find any _____ in London after he left university.

## Vocabulary: multi-word verbs with *cut*

SB p.180

Complete the sentences with *cut* + a preposition.

1 If we don't pay our bill then they might _____ our electricity.

2 Simon _____ the meat into little pieces for his dog.

3 My grandmother _____ the pieces of the dress and started to sew them together.

4 We must _____ on how much water we use by having showers instead of baths.

## Use of English: future passive

SB p.180

1 Write the words in the correct order to make sentences.

1 space. / Robots / going to be / next month / are / sent into /

_____

2 done / By the 2030s, / a lot of / by robots. / be / will / our jobs

_____

3 won't / used / some countries. / be / in / These machines

_____

**4** sold / This robot / isn't / to be / any more. / going

_____

**5** driven / to be / Are we / going / by a robot car / tomorrow?

_____

**6** found / on / Will / life / other planets? / be

_____

**2** **Choose the correct options to complete the text.**

---

**NEW ROBOTS ON SALE!**

Next week, two brand new robots are going on sale! The first robot is

going to ¹ _____ called Tidybot and it's going to be

² _____ to do housework. The second robot is going to be

³ _____ as Chefbot and this one is going ⁴ _____ used

to cook food and prepare drinks too! Sit back and relax and let the

robots do your work for you!

Inventor of the robots, Julia Zane, said, "we're confident that people will

like the new robots and we think that many homes ⁵ _____ be

transformed by Tidybot and Chefbot!" Experts think that over 100 000

robots will be ⁶ _____ by the end of the year.

---

| **1** | **a** being | **b** been | **c** be | **d** is |
|---|---|---|---|---|
| **2** | **a** use | **b** used | **c** using | **d** user |
| **3** | **a** know | **b** knew | **c** knowing | **d** known |
| **4** | **a** to | **b** be | **c** to be | **d** to being |
| **5** | **a** we'll | **b** will | **c** willing | **d** wheel |
| **6** | **a** sell | **b** sold | **c** selling | **d** sale |

**3** **Change the spelling in the sentences so that it is correct in British English.**

**1** In the future, the world will be controled by robots. _____

**2** This robot will never be equaled. _____

**3** This road will be traveled by many students. _____

**4** I think that tomorrow's meeting will be canceled. _____

**1** **Look again at the text and answer the questions.**

**1** How would you describe the character of Dr Frankenstein?

_____

**2** What different settings are there in this extract?

_____

**3** What different feelings does Dr Frankenstein have during this extract?

_____

**4** How do you think the creature might feel?

_____

**2** **Answer the questions.**

**1** What things can you do to create excitement in a story?

_____

**2** What did you enjoy about reading this extract of _Frankenstein_?

_____

**3** Would you like to read the rest of the book? Why? Why not?

_____

**Check your progress**

**1 What can you do now?**

I can …

listen to a conversation about robot workers ☐

use nouns + prepositions ☐

use the future passive ☐

read an article about the future of robots, discuss and write about the subject ☐

read an extract from Mary Shelley's _Frankenstein_ ☐

design a new robot ☐

**My learning**
What did you learn in this unit?

**2 Answer the questions about this unit.**

**1** What have you enjoyed most?

_____

**2** Is there anything you have found difficult?

_____

**3** What would you like to learn more about?

_____

# End-of-year review

## Vocabulary: word hunt

**Find four**

jobs

social media sites

technological devices

phrases you see in shop signs

compound adjectives

abstract nouns

adverbs

multi-word verbs

## Vocabulary: a crossword puzzle

**Complete the crossword.**

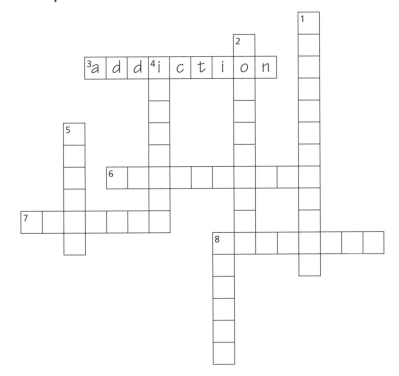

**Across**

3 when someone can't stop doing something that is bad for him / her

6 a place in a city where you can look at paintings or drawings

7 a person who writes a blog

8 a person that you don't know

**Down**

1 when people want to work but can't because there aren't enough jobs for them

2 a person who writes news stories

4 the person who has the idea for an invention

5 a plastic or cardboard box for food or drink

8 the money you get for doing a job

## Writing: punctuation

**Rewrite the sentences, adding in the missing punctuation and capital letters.**

**1** lets go and see a concert this weekend said sarah

_____

**2** sorry i cant im doing a run to support a local charity replied danny

_____

**3** thats great said sarah what charity are you supporting

_____

**4** its a charity that helps disabled people do sports

_____

**5** sarah said well done danny im proud of you

_____

## Writing: spelling

**Underline and correct the spelling mistake in each sentence. One sentence has no mistakes.**

**1** Sam is very confidant and generous. _____

**2** This is possibly the best day of my life! _____

**3** He opened his present immediatly. _____

**4** He bought three loafs of bread because they were on special offer. _____

**5** When I grow up I want to be an inventer. _____

**6** We have traveled a long way to be here. _____

## Writing: my year

**Think about what you have learned this year in English and complete the sentences.**

**1** My favourite topic of the book was _____ because _____

_____.

**2** I think that I am good at _____.

**3** I think that I need more practice in _____.

**4** This year in English, I am proud of myself because I have made progress with

_____.

**5** Next year in English, I would like to learn how to _____.

# Focus on grammar

## 1 Present and past continuous tenses

a. The present continuous tense
   - is made with *am/is/are* + *-ing* form of the verb
   - is used to talk about actions that are continuing in the present
b. The past continuous tense
   - is made with *was/were* + *-ing* form of the verb
   - is used to talk about actions that were continuing in the present

*See Section 6 for passive forms of these tenses.*

## 2 Present perfect simple tense

The present perfect tense

- is made with *have/has* (*not*) + past participle of the verb.
- links the past and the present. The action takes place in the past but there is always a connection with *now*.

The present perfect tense has three uses.

a. for something that *has happened recently*

   We sometimes use *just* when we talk about the recent past.

   *The players have just arrived.*

b. for something that started in the past and is still not finished

   We often use *for* and *since* when we talk about the unfinished past.
   - Use *since* with a point in time.

   *Scientists have known about Komodo dragons since 1916.*
   - Use *for* with a period of time.

   *They have studied these strange creatures for over a hundred years.*

c. for an experience

   We often use *ever* in questions and *never* in answers when we talk about experiences.

   *Have you ever seen a Komodo dragon?*

   *No, I've never seen one in real life but I've seen them on television.*

We often use time adverbs with the present perfect.

- yet = at any time up to now     *I haven't seen the new film **yet**.*
- just = a short time ago     *I've **just** seen the new film.*
- ever = at any time up to now     *Have you **ever** seen this film?*
- never = at no time up to now     *I've **never** seen the film.*

*See Section 15 for more about adverbs.*

## 3 Present perfect continuous tense

The present perfect continuous tense

- is made with (*have/has*) *not* + *been* + *-ing* form of the verb.
- links the past and the present. The action takes place in the past but there is always a connection with now. There is an emphasis on the process as well as the result.

The present perfect continuous tense is used:

a. for something that started in the past and continues in the present
   *Sarah has been waiting for a bus for three hours.*
b. for something that has just finished but we're interested in the results
   *I've been looking for you for two hours.*

We often use the present perfect continuous with *How long ...?*
   *How long have you been living here?*
   *I've been living here for four years.*

## 4 Past perfect tense

The past perfect tense

- is made with *had* (*not*) + past particple
- is used to talk about an earlier past (i.e. two steps into the past)
   *By six o'clock yesterday, I had finished all my work.*
- is often used with the past simple tense
   *Before I went to Paris last month, I had flown in a plane only once.*

## 5 Future forms

There are four ways to talk about the future in English:

She | *will arrive*
*is going to arrive*
*is arriving*
*arrives* | *tomorrow evening at 19.00.*

All of the sentences are correct. However, there are some differences in the use of each.

a. **will** + verb is used for
- sudden decisions (often with *I think*)
   *I think I'll talk to my teacher tomorrow.*      *I'm tired. I think I'll go to bed.*
- predicting or guessing
   *In the future we will all go to university.*      *I think it will rain tomorrow*
- future events you are certain about
   *It will be my birthday next week.*      *The teacher will be here in a minute.*
b. **be going to** + verb is used for
- something we have decided to do, or plans
   *I'm **going to fly** to Lagos tomorrow.*      *He's **going to visit** us on Friday.*
- future events we have evidence for
   *Look at the sky! It's **going to rain**.*      *Look at the time! We're **going to be** late.*
c. The **present continuous tense** is used for
- fixed or firm plans - often with a time, date or place
   *I'm **meeting** him at six o'clock at the airport.*      *They're **arriving** on Monday.*

d. The **present simple tense** is used for
- things which are timetabled to happen in the future

  *His plane **arrives** at 08.30. What time does the exam **begin** tomorrow?*

See Section 6 for passive forms of these tenses.

## 6 Passive forms

- A passive can be used with any of the verb tenses: we use the verb *be* in the appropriate tense + past participle. Some examples:

| | | | | |
|---|---|---|---|---|
| PRESENT SIMPLE PASSIVE: | The *film* | *is* | *chosen* | *by the manager.* |
| PRESENT CONTINUOUS PASSIVE: | *The book* | *is being* | *written.* | |
| PAST SIMPLE PASSIVE: | *The car* | *was* | *washed* | *by my sister.* |
| FUTURE WITH *will*: | *We* | *will be* | *followed.* | |
| FUTURE WITH *going to*: | *We* | *are going to be* | *followed.* | |

- We use passives when we don't know, we don't want to say or it is not important who did something. Passives are often used in reports.

  *My money was stolen. (I don't know who took it.)*

  *A lot of rice is eaten in Asia. (It is not important who eats it.)*
- When we use a passive and want to say who did something, we use *by ...*

  *A telephone call was made by my mother.*

## 7 Modal verbs

- Modal verbs add meaning to main verbs. They are not used about facts. They are used to express ability, possibility, certainty, requests, suggestions, necessity, etc.
- The modal verbs are *can, could, may, might, must, shall, should, will, would, ought to*. We also use *have to* and *need to* for the same purpose.
- Past modal verbs *should/shouldn't have* are used to express regret and criticism.
- We use modal verbs before main verbs and in short answers.

  *You must hurry up.     Can you wait a minute?     No, I can't?*
- Modal verbs only have one form (they do not add *-s, -ing* or *-ed*).
- After a modal we use the simple form of the main verb.

  *You may go.     We should wait.*
- Modal verbs do not need *do/does/did* in questions.

  *Could you help me? (NOT ~~Do you could help me?~~)*

## 8 The unlikely conditional – with *if/unless/if only/wish that*

The unlikely conditional
- is used to talk about the result of things which are not likely to happen.

  *If it snowed, I would be surprised.     I'd be very happy if I had my own plane.*
- has two clauses.
  - The *If* clause has a verb in the simple past tense.
  - The main clause has *would* (or *wouldn't*) and a verb in the simple form.

    *If it rained, we would be happy.  They wouldn't believe me if I said that you were here.*

- can replace *if + not* with *unless*.

  *If it wasn't safe, I wouldn't take you. = Unless it was safe, I wouldn't take you.*
- can be used to give advice.

  *If I were you, I would see a doctor tomorrow.*
- can be used to express a wish.

  *If I had lots of money, I would buy my mother a car.*

  *If only/wish that*
- can be used with the past perfect to express regret and criticism.

  *If only I had arrived on time.*      *If only I hadn't eaten all that cake.*

  *I wish I had arrived on time.*      *I wish I hadn't eaten all that cake.*

## 9 Reported speech

- When we use reported speech the place, time and speaker has usually changed from the time and place that the words were spoken. For this reason we often have to change the verb tenses, pronouns and 'time and place' words.
- The tenses change like this:

| tense change | speaking | reported speech |
|---|---|---|
| present simple ➜ past simple | "I **walk** to school." | He said he **walked** to school. |
| present continuous ➜ past continuous | "He **is working**." | She said he **was working**. |
| past simple ➜ past perfect | "I **played** football." | He said he **had played** football. |
| present perfect ➜ past perfect | "We **have missed** school every day." | I said we **had missed** school every day. |

- Examples of how time and place words change:

| | | |
|---|---|---|
| *now* | ➜ | *then* |
| *today* | ➜ | *that day* |
| *yesterday* | ➜ | *the day before* |
| *tomorrow* | ➜ | *the next day* |
| *next week/month/year* | ➜ | *the following week/month/year* |
| *last week/month/year* | ➜ | *the week/month/year before* |
| *here* | ➜ | *there* |

- When we report on a situation that has not changed (the time and place are still the same) then we do not have to change the verb tense. This happens when:
  - we repeat something immediately after it is said:

    *"He is arriving soon."*      *"What did you say?"*      *"I said he is arriving soon."*
  - we are talking about something which is still true or always true:

    *"My name is William."*      *He said his name is William.*

    *"Water boils at 100°C."*      *The teacher told us that water boils at 100°C.*

- The most common verbs for reporting are *said* and *told*. There is an important difference in the way they are used.
    - ○ We use *told* when we say **who** somebody is talking to.
      *Adu **told his wife** that there was a problem. I **told you** that I would help.*
    - ○ We use *said* in other cases.
      ***Adu said** that there was a problem. **I said** that we would meet later.*
- To report a command, use *told* + noun/pronoun + *to* + verb.
  *The teacher said, "Cal, sit down."*
  *The teacher told Cal to sit down.*
- To report a request, use *asked* + noun/pronoun + *to* + verb.
  *Jan said, "Help me carry this box, please."*
  *Jan asked me to help him carry a box.*
- To report a *Wh-question*, use *asked* and the word order of a statement (not a question). Do not use a question mark.
  *He said, "Where are you going?"*
  *The man asked where I was going.*
- To report a *yes/no* question, use *asked* + *if*.
  *My mother said, "Are you feeling well?"*
  *My mother asked if I was feeling well.*

*See Section 11 for polite questions inside statements or questions.*

## 10 Relative clauses

- Relative clauses are used to give information about a noun. They allow us to make sentences longer and more interesting.
- There are two types of relative clauses:
a. A **defining relative clause** tells us who or what the noun is. It is an important part of a sentence. If we take it out we might not know what the noun is we are talking about.
  *The doctor **who you saw yesterday** is away today.*
b. A **non-defining relative clause** gives us extra information about the noun. We can take it out of the sentence and still understand it. We use commas to separate it from the rest of the sentence.
  *The doctor, **who is now over 70**, is resting.*
- The first word of a relative clause is usually a relative pronoun.
    - ○ **who** – refers to a person
        - o *I saw a man **who** has a wooden leg.*
    - ○ **which** – refers to an animal or a thing
        - o *There is the dog **which** bit me.*
    - ○ **that** – can replace *who* and *which* to refer to a person, animal or thing
        - o *I saw a man **that** has a wooden leg.  There is the dog **that** bit me*
- Relative pronouns replace other pronouns in the relative clause – don't use both.
  *My mother has a friend who ~~she~~ is a singer.*

- We can use *why* in a relative clause to give reasons.
  *The reason **why** I like her is that she always has time to help.*
- We can use *where* in a relative clause to talk about a place.
  *This is the place **where** I live.*
- We can use *when* in a relative clause to talk about a time.
  *2015 was the year **when** my brother was born.*
- We can use *whose* in a relative clause to talk about possession.
  *This is the boy **whose** coat I borrowed.*
- We can use prepositions in relative clauses. In formal English, they go before the relative pronoun and in informal English, they go at the end of the sentence.
  *New York is the city **from** where my friend comes.*
  *New York is the city where my friend comes **from**.*

  *Ben Marsh is the man **to** whom the prize was given.*
  *Ben Marsh is the man who the prize was given **to**.*

## 11 Question forms

- We can use prepositions in questions, too. In formal English, they go before the question word and in informal English, they go at the end of the sentence.
  *__At__ what time did the lesson start?*     *What time did the lesson start **at**?*
  *__In__ which direction did Mel go?*     *Which direction did Mel go **in**?*
  *__From__ whose class is this student?*     *Whose class is this student **from**?*
- When we want to ask a question politely, we can put it inside another question or statement.
  Direct question: *What time did he arrive?*
  Indirect questions: *__Could you tell me__ what time he arrived?*
  *__I wonder__ if you could tell me what time he arrived.*
  *__Do you know__ what time he arrived?*

## 12 *to* + verb after adjectives and verbs

- After adjectives, we use *to* + verb.
  *I'm shocked to hear the news.   We're likely to stay for dinner. He's certain to arrive on time.*
- After some verbs, we use *to* + verb.
  *I promise to help you.     He appears to be happy.*

## 13 *-ing* forms after prepositions and verbs

- After a preposition, we use the *-ing* form of a verb.
  *I dream about becoming a vet.     Are you interested in studying French?*
- After some verbs, we use the *-ing* form of a verb.
  *He suggested talking to you.     He avoided sitting in the sun.*

# 14 Pronouns

- Pronouns take the place of nouns, e.g. *she, it, them, ours.*
- We use **indefinite pronouns** when we don't know, or don't want to say, exactly who or what we are talking about:

| everybody | everyone | everything |
|-----------|----------|------------|
| somebody | someone | something |
| anybody | anyone | anything |
| nobody | no one | nothing |

- We use **demonstrative pronouns** when we want to indicate what we're talking about by pointing at something.

  *This is beautiful.   That is my son.   These are my choices.   Those are my shoes.*

  These pronouns can also be used to refer to something that has just been mentioned in a sentence.

  *I don't feel very well.   This is why I don't want to go out.*

  *He gave me chocolates and flowers.   These were my birthday presents.*

# 15 Adverbs

- Adverbs give information about *how, where, when* or *how often* an action happens, or *how certain* we are that it will happen.

  *You always laugh. He is certainly waiting for us. I can never eat this.*

- Adverbs that tell us *how, where* and *when* usually go at the end of a sentence. There can be more than one adverb in a sentence. The order for these adverbs is *how – where – when.*

  *They played well in the match yesterday.*

- Adverbs that tell us *when* can also go at the beginning of a sentence. We use a comma after the adverb. This gives the adverb more importance.

  *I will help you when you arrive. When you arrive, I will help you.*

- Adverbs that tell us *how often* or *how certain* go before a main verb, and after a modal or *is/are/was/were/do/does/did.*

- Some adverbs describe the whole sentence rather than a particular verb and these come at the end of a sentence.

  *I loved this book, so I would like to read the sequel as well.* (to add information)

  *I loved this book, but I didn't like the sequel though.* (to add contrasting information)

# 16 Comparing

- When we compare with adjectives we can make the comparison stronger or weaker by using structures like *not as* + adjective + *as, just as* + adjective + *as, much* + comparative adjective + *than, slightly* + comparative adjective + *than.*

  *I'm not as tall as you.   He's just as tall as you.*

  *He's much stronger than he was.   He's slightly stronger than he was.*

- When we compare with adverbs we can make the comparison stronger or weaker by using structures like *not as* + adverb + *as*, *just as* + adverb + *as*, *far less/more* + adverb, *much* + comparative adverb + *than*, *slightly* + comparative adverb + *than*.

  *This computer doesn't work as quickly as it used to.   Sarah runs just as quickly as Max.*
  *You drive far more carefully than your father.   It rained much more heavily than last week.*
  *The children sang slightly louder than they did before.*

- We use *like* or *as* to say one thing is the same as another. They are called similes.
  - verb + *like* + noun phrase: *She's like a second mother to me. It disappeared like ice in the sun.*
  - *as* + adjective + *as*: *It was as cold as ice.  He ran as fast as a cheetah.*

# 17 Connectives

- Connectives connect two ideas within a sentence or across sentences.
  - Some always go between the two ideas, e.g. *and, or, but, so.*
  - Others can go between the two ideas or at the beginning of the sentence. If the connective is at the beginning of the sentence, use a comma between the two ideas.

  *Although I like flying, I didn't enjoy that journey*

- We use *so that* and *(in order) to* to explain a purpose.
  - *I studied hard **so that** I would do well in my exam.*
  - *We opened the window **(in order) to** let some air in.*

- We use *although* and *though* to contrast two ideas:
  - ***Although** I don't have a lot of free time, I always make time to read in the evenings.*
  - *I don't usually like non-fiction, **though** I love reading autobiographies.*

- We use *while* to balance two contrasting ideas.
  - ***While** I don't enjoy comedy, my sister loves it.*
  - *I always read quickly, **while** my friend reads slowly.*